ANDRÉ VILLAS-BOAS

ANDRÉ VILLAS-BOAS
SPECIAL TOO

LUÍS MIGUEL PEREIRA & JAIME PINHO

foreword by
LUÍS FREITAS LOBO

dewi lewis media

ANDRÉ VILLAS-BOAS: SPECIAL TOO
by LUÍS MIGUEL PEREIRA & JAIME PINHO

This edition first published in the UK in 2011 by
Dewi Lewis Media Ltd
8, Broomfield Road
Heaton Moor
Stockport SK4 4ND
www.dewilewismedia.com

Original publication in Portugal in September 2011 by Prime Books

Editors: Dewi Lewis & Caroline Warhurst
Translation: sintagma traduções, lda
Design and Artwork Production: Dewi Lewis Media Ltd
Print and binding: Gutenberg Press, Malta

ISBN: 978-1-905928-08-8

10   9   8   7   6   5   4   3   2   1

CONTENTS

FOREWORD

HOW FOOTBALL ANTICIPATES SCIENCE

*"I prefer inspired perspiration to momentary
inspiration, talent to strength, the action of effort
to the over-performance of sacrifice."*

Marcelo Bielsa

André Villas-Boas is an impulsive coach for whom science is a starting point; he is an architect of the theory of chaos as it is applied to football – that "chaotic and emotional game" which is decoded every 90 minutes through tactics and strategies which reveal themselves through "rehearsed improvisations". There are no contradictions in any of this. Or rather, not when it is applied to the world of football, and particularly to the advanced, modern approach to the game. Conflict and collaboration. They may appear to be opposites, but in football it makes no sense for them not to co-exist.

Villas-Boas grew up thinking about football, about the "transitions" that take place in a game, and about the secrets of "formations". When his job was to analyse information about opposing teams, each report that he undertook – whether of a team or an individual – was, for him, like an "x-ray" of whoever was under observation. The "tactical head" of each player was opened up and put to the service of a coaching staff who had now become focussed on "scientific football".

His own concept of the game developed as a result of this, he drew upon many influences, learning and questioning the various methodologies. He followed Capello's theory of "the best coach as the greatest of thieves", all the while moulding his own philo-sophy of football – a philosophy which is always open to heated discussion. This is the style of the coach and of the human being, the "football animal" that is André Villas-Boas, with his need to debate and discuss football "seriously". Also ever-present in his mind is the respect that each team should have for the ball; and the central ambition that tactics should be seen as the engine to move the ball around the pitch.

The quote at the beginning of this chapter is one of André Villas-Boas's favourites. It mirrors some of the complexity of the factors I have mentioned. He and I had a mutual admiration of Marcelo 'El Loco' Bielsa [1] and the quote was one that André and I texted each other about at the time he was given the opportunity (at Académica) to begin his career as a manager. To say this is not to betray a confidence but rather to confirm my belief that this quote reflects much of his ideology of the game, bringing together elements such as inspiration and perspiration, talent and effort, without turning them into enemies. The game and a team, need all of these elements to be able to come to life on the pitch.

To speak of André Villas-Boas simply in terms of a tactical approach is limiting. No tactical formation has a life of its own; it depends on the dynamics given to it. And therefore, to speak of his dedication to the 4-3-3 formation is to speak only of a devotion to a diagram. The "personalisation" of that system is missing. As an assistant coach with "x-ray" vision, he spoke of his move to Inter with José Mourinho as an enticing challenge – the challenge to win in Italy with a different idea of football from that defined by the transalpine "old testament". To win with a high-pressure 4-3-3 strategy, instead of the speculative football typical of the Italian school. Whether or not that actually happened, is an entirely different matter. André Villas-Boas, the coach, was yet to come into his own.

Apart from the results achieved, his year at FC Porto (2010/11)

---

1. Marcelo 'the madman' Bielsa is a former national team coach for both Argentina and Chile. He is currently the manager of Athletic Bilbao.

was marked by the constant need and desire to repeat that his team was "a possession team", and to view controlled "transitions" as his instrument of choice during the different stages of a game. In other words, as a means of securing particular formations (defensive and, above all, attacking) as a result of these transitions.

At the end of his time at Porto he dedicated his victories to Bobby Robson, for the passion he transmitted; to José Mourinho, for the opportunities given; and to Pep Guardiola, for the ideology he holds to. It is the third "dedication" that sets out his view of the game. To have possession of the ball and move it around the entire pitch in an organised way, with technical skill, and with a team that is patient in the way it searches out and creates space to allow it to penetrate the opponents' defence. Even when he was managing a lower level team such as Académica, who were struggling to avoid relegation, he still sought to carry out these ideas on the pitch – even at a time when the extreme importance of achieving results must have been an almost primal instinct.

His FC Porto were seen as the "high definition" of that idea that had been present since his first days as manager. As he fine-tuned approaches and communication skills in and outside the group, his "4-3-3 possession football" was taking shape on the pitch and, above all, in the minds of great players. There were those who needed a great deal of time spent explaining it to them – and those who only needed a word or two.

It is impossible to resist the temptation of comparing Villas-Boas' 2011 season at FC Porto with that of Mourinho's first in 2003, when they also won the European League (the then UEFA Cup). There are indeed some similarities. For some 'scholars' it really was Mourinho's best team, at least as far as the attractiveness of the football was concerned. I agree with that. It was a period during which the team not only played a high pressure 4-3-3 formation, but also had midfield creativity.

The following season, the one in which Porto went on to win the

Champions League, the decision was taken to move to a 4-4-2 diamond formation. During Villa-Boas's year at Porto his 'blue-and-white machine' expressed itself through 4-3-3 and also had a roaming forward winger who liked to make diagonal runs (in many ways Hulk[2] played this role in AVB's team, just as Derlei[3] had in Mourinho's team). Different players in value (both on the pitch and in the transfer market) and in their ability to break forward, but who offered similar ways to set up the team and its attacking dynamics. The Villas-Boas midfield didn't have a player like Deco[4], but it had gained an increased defence-attack-defence movement with Moutinho[5]. The importance given to the defensive midfielder was similar, but Villas-Boas aimed for him to 'play more' when in possession of the ball. Mourinho's full-backs defended better. Those of Villas-Boas tended to break forward more, to unbalance the opponent rather than to provide support. However, at Porto, I believe the differences actually stemmed from individual characteristics rather than from 'team play' options. As a striker, Falcao[6] brought a new dimension to the position, and at the back there wasn't a player with the charisma and the roar of a centre-back 'à la Porto'. Instead, Villas-Boas worked with two centre-backs for an increased sense of positional stability.

We will never know what Villas-Boas's second season at FC Porto would have been like. I don't believe he would have evolved

---

2. *Brazilian born, Givanildo Vieira de Souza, known as Hulk, joined Porto in 2008. He plays primarily on the right wing but also as a striker.*
3. *Brazilian born striker, Vanderlei Fernandes Silva, known as Derlei, was in Mourinho's team at Leiria where he scored 21 goals in the 2001/2 season. He joined Porto when Mourinho moved there.*
4. *Brazilian born, Deco (Anderson Luís de Souza) is one of the few players to have won the UEFA Champions League with two different clubs – Porto in 2004 and FC Barcelona in 2006. He moved to Chelsea in 2008 as the first signing of Luiz Felipe Scolari.*
5. *A Portuguese international, João Moutinho joined Porto in 2010. Mainly a central midfielder, he is a versatile player who can also operate as a holding or attacking midfielder, and on either flank.*
6. *Radamel Falcao García Zárate, known as Falcao, is a Colombian striker currently playing for Atlético Madrid. He scored 41 goals in 51 appearances for Porto in 2009/2011.*

(or rather, transformed) the system towards the diamond shape, however, there were clues in several of his games on the Porto bench which indicated a willingness, on occasion, to play with four midfielders, or more accurately, four men in the midfield. And so, rather than looking to dominate the game he sought (and managed) to control it. This may seem the same but it is very different. Basically, with more men in the midfield and by giving more width to the diamond, the team could move the ball more and do so more calmly. That was the moment when Villas-Boas referred to the team as "resting with the ball". It was an idea that had already emerged from "Mourinho's books" and one that André Villas-Boas succeeded in understanding and adapting to his game concept. More than playing in different systems, what is important is to know how to change systems throughout the game.

When a goal doesn't come, the solution is rarely to increase the number of players in the opponents's penalty box. On the contrary, it is to better work on developing play further back, in midfield areas and "between lines" so as to create opportunities. A steady build up before the realisation, both in the way that it is thought about and later when it is applied to the game. Obviously there can often be a problem of a lack of players in the box, but, in the overall ideology of how to approach any match, this is how a team should think. This is how a top football team should play.

The need to understand each player is in direct proportion to understanding how he can be important to the team. In that context, Guarín[7] felt an 'improvement' in his football. More than any improvement in him as a player though, what changed was what was required of him in the game. Instead of only pressing forward in a defensive way and then having a recovery role, he went on to having a broader tactical responsibility, increasing the setting up of play as well as leading it and later moving into shooting areas. So, within

---

7. *Colombian midfield player, Fredy Guarín joined Porto in 2008.*

the 4-3-3 formation, the role of the No. 6 stopped being one of a defensive pivot and became that of a pivot, full stop. Underlying this is a game concept in which, besides him being seen as a guarantee of defensive balance – something which is indispensable in that position – he is also given other roles such as initiating forward breaks, which begin by him retreating between the centre-backs who then move further apart, while the full-backs move up almost to the halfway line. In this way a better tactical and technical quality of play can be initiated.

At the base of his 4-3-3 'tactic' was the movement off the ball which was interpreted as being the search for empty spaces to provide options and pass lines to whoever had the ball. Players being able to see each other, and thus giving each other options as to what to do with the ball. That is the best interpretation of the so-called "principles of the game" (by definition this relates to behavioural references that players have on the pitch as to what they should do in certain situations or spaces). Running yes, but with criteria ('inspired perspiration' as was quoted earlier).

In his 'ten commandments' of ball possession Villas-Boas prefers, as a 'fundamental commandment', that players hold on to the ball rather than the speculative attitude of waiting to recover the ball then breaking fast towards the opponent's goal (the so-called quick transitions). Instead of four or five swift long passes, Villas-Boas doesn't mind if his team take 14 or 15 short and squarer ones, until they reach the opponent's area, making use of depth at the right moment, holding on to the ball as long as possible so that there is less need to win it back. Even if it means that to get the shape of the team right there is the need for a back-pass or to pass the ball around at the back. The home crowd at Porto's Dragon Stadium gradually realised that this, an apparently excessive passing game, was merely a means to start building an attack. Persuading fans to be patient – by nature they are intolerant of a team which seems slow in taking the initiative to attack the opposing team – is I believe the greatest triumph for a manager other than achieving the right results. It is also the most difficult. André Villas-Boas accomplished this with his '4-3-3 of ball possession and movement' and, when necessary, the use of a high defence line and vigorous ball recovery.

And, of course, he also won all the titles.

In the result-geared times that we live in, the victory of aesthetics over pragmatism is an 'author's triumph'. It is also a priority for the tactical health of the football world. This is the football of André Villas-Boas.

Luís Freitas Lobo

1

THE MONARCH OF FOOTBALL

*"He had a great desire to learn, especially about the tactical
aspects, and the presence of Robson in his character was
very clear. If, as a manager, he can combine the organisation
of Mourinho and the attacking football of Robson,
then he will be very good indeed."*

George Burley [8]

André Villas-Boas or rather Dom Luís André de Pina Cabral e
Villas-Boas. This is the name under which Chelsea's manager
appears on his family's genealogical tree. This noble title – granted
by King D. Carlos I, in 1890 – dates back to his paternal great
grandfather, José Gerardo Coelho Vieira Pinto do Vale Peixoto de
Villas-Boas (1863-1913), the first Viscount of Guidhomil. Alfredo
(1825-1906), José Gerardo's brother, was the Count of Paço de
Vieira – in the north of Portugal, close to Guimarães. He was a
judge and an influential figure in the government of the then Prime
Minister Ernesto Hintze Ribeiro, working as Minister for Public
Works and as the civil governor of Ponta Delgada in the Azores.
And before them, José Gerardo and Alfredo's father, José Joaquim
Villas-Boas (1825-1906) had been the Baron of Paço de Vieira and
the civil governor of Braga.

Gonçalo, the youngest son of the first Viscount of Guidhomil
and grandfather to André Villas-Boas, married Margaret Neville
Kendall, whose mother's family – the Burns – were from Lancashire
and Merseyside. The Portuguese connection comes about through

---

8. George Burley was Ipswich manager during André Villas-Boas's placement at the club.

Margaret's father's family, the Kendalls, who had been in Portugal for at least four generations, and were most likely connected with the Port wine industry. It was through this grandmother, Margaret, born in Lordelo de Ouro, that Villas-Boas took his first steps towards learning English, mastering the language at an early age. And as fate would have it, three decades later André would himself return to the place of departure, the country and birthplace of grandmother Margaret.

The current Chelsea manager enjoyed a wealthy childhood. His parents, Teresa and Luis Filipe, were an upper-middle class family, who lived close to the famed Avenida da Boavista. Luis Filipe, professor and chemical engineer, studied in Portugal before moving to England, where he completed his doctorate at the Chemistry Faculty of the University of Kent, Canterbury. André Villas-Boas's father is currently a lecturer at the Chemical Engineering Faculty of Lisbon's Technical University, Universidade Técnica de Lisboa and works for a company that supplies car parts for Volkswagen, Audi, Seat and Skoda. His mother, Teresa, has her own clothing business, with a number of shops in Porto.

Teresa and Luís Filipe married in 1973, four years before André was born. They always ensured that their children had the very best education and André attended the Colégio do Rosário, one of the most expensive private schools in Porto and with a reputation for academic excellence. Founded on deeply religious principles, the Colégio Sagrado Coração de Maria (the Sacred Heart of Mary School) came into being at the turn of the 20th century as a result of a merger with the former English School (yet another British detail in André's story). It was originally run by an Irish nun, Miss Hennessey, and other members of the Order of the Sacred Heart of Mary. However, following a proclamation by the Republic of Portugal on 5 October 1910, a decree came into force forbidding religious orders from teaching, and subsequently there was an exodus of nuns. However, it was not sufficient to remove the religious basis of the School and consequently André Villas-Boas was exposed to strongly religious principles during his childhood.

FOOTBALL ON THE TIP OF HIS TONGUE

Early on it became quite clear that André wasn't the type to see his aristocratic background as something to isolate him from the rest of the world or to make him special. When he looked in the mirror, it wasn't a face of noble descent that he saw. Other than his ginger hair, which led his classmates to nickname him "little carrot", everything else about him was ordinary. His childhood was much the same as that of any other child. He was easy-going, quiet and affable. His school grades were fine, but not great. He was always an average student.

André would only get really excited when the subject was football, always revealing an out of the ordinary sharpness of wit, as well as an irreverence. He knew everything: players and coaches, clubs and transfers, promising players and those who had taken on an almost sacred status. In the courtyard of the Colégio do Rosário, he was always ready for any discussion, with the winning argument on the tip of his tongue.

Strangely enough, however, there were no fervent football fans in the family. His vast knowledge of the subject came from extensive reading of sports newspapers, football sticker collections and an invaluable computer game: *Championship Manager*. It was his first bench. He'd sign players, decide on his eleven and make his substitutions. The famous game left an indelible impression on many teenagers of the 1980s, but for André it ran much deeper than that: this was a game that pointed to his future profession. He would type away furiously on the keyboard, totally enthralled – he had the world at his fingertips! Later, the names of his heroes could be found in his school notebooks, scribbles about football tactics instead of Portuguese or arithmetic. Perhaps this obsession goes some way to explain why he was classified as an "average" student.

His fascination with football was only matched by his passion for FC Porto. Unbiased witnesses confirm that when André Villas-Boas went to school he would take with him exhaustive technical and tactical reports on the team. Each Monday, he would pull out his notes and earnestly discuss the weekend's game.

On 4 July 1980, at the age of only two and a half, he had become a member of FC Porto. He has remained one ever since. His membership number is 11, 428, and time has only strengthened his passion. He was a constant presence at the Antas Stadium (FC Porto's former grounds), where he would watch matches and look in on training sessions. In May 1987, when the team played in, and won, their first European Cup Final, André Villas-Boas, aged only nine, celebrated FC Porto's victory together with his family at his grandmother's home. That European title meant so much to him that, had he been allowed to, he would have gone to Prater Stadium that very day to pull out a tuft of grass as a memento. Little did he know that 24 years later, he himself would be living that very same European dream, as manager of his favourite team.

MESSAGES FOR BOBBY ROBSON

Teresa Maria and Luis Filipe followed the course of the second of their four children (two girls and two boys) with a degree of anticipation, perhaps even trepidation. At an early age it was already possible to see how difficult it would be to put a brake on such strong impulses. To deprive him of football or FC Porto would have been tantamount to robbing him of his happiness; it would certainly have wiped away his boyish smile. And so, with the family's consent, André continued signing, selling, building and boosting imaginary squads, with a view to a career in sports journalism –perhaps.

André continued building his sandcastles in the air, until one day reality moved in... next door. He was 16 years old, when fate decided that his neighbours, in the very same apartment block, would be the Robson family – Bobby[9] and his wife, Elsie. No more, no less than the newly-signed manager of FC Porto.

André viewed this as the opportunity of a lifetime. One day, taking advantage of a chance encounter, he approached the British manager with a pertinent – even provocative – question. In the English that he had been taught by his grandmother Margaret, he asked Robson why he was leaving his idol Domingos Paciência, a promising Porto striker, on the bench so often. Instead of reprimanding such arrogance, Robson responded with a smile, revealing an openness of mind that is not commonly found.

Contact between the young Villas-Boas and Sir Bobby became more frequent. André would regularly leave reports and tactical notes in Robson's post box, and the coach would respond with various incentives. "He gave me the opportunity to observe FC Porto training sessions. I was just a Porto supporter and that was fantastic," admitted André Villas-Boas recently. André also began to pay frequent visits to the Foz English Club and other clubs, always as a guest of Bobby Robson.

The truth is that this socialising proved decisive in determining the future options available to the teenage André. Making allowance for the impulsiveness of youth, Robson was impressed by the passion and competence of the young boy. And so, he gave him credit by accepting his "homework", and even using it at times, or at least taking note of it. Only much later did the rest of the coaching staff, including the then interpreter, José Mourinho, meet young André. For the moment, things remained between the wise coach and the inquisitive youngster.

The decision had been taken. André Villas-Boas would enter the

---

9. *Bobby Robson was manager at FC Porto from 1994 to 1996.*

footballing world through hands-on experience, and with the support of one of the greatest figures in world football, Bobby Robson, to boot. For around a year he attended the best possible faculty – just like a fairy tale for him – the training sessions, seeing his idols, the reports, the statistics, the clubs… André took it all in, like a sponge, as if there were no tomorrow.

He was 17 when he gave up on his university course and set out on his future vocation. Following Bobby Robson's suggestion, he went to England to begin his training as a coach. At Lilleshall he took what would be the first of a number of courses. In 1997, he continued his studies at the Scottish Football Association (SFA), while at the same time undertaking internships at professional clubs, such as Ipswich. George Burley, Ipswich manager at the time, remembers the young student well: "Robson called me and asked if I could have a young coaching candidate over, let him watch training and show him how the club worked for a few weeks." Bobby Robson had a great influence on André, and this was very much apparent during his internship at Ipswich. "He had a great desire to learn, especially about the tactical aspects, and the presence of Robson in his character was very clear. If, as a manager, he can combine the organisation of Mourinho and the attacking football of Robson, then he will be very good indeed," concludes George Burley.

He did his C, B, A and Pro Licences at the Scottish Football Association, always in a very committed way. "He was very dedicated and studious, devouring everything he could get his hands on, such as books on psychology and physiology," says Jim Fleeting, SFA director of football development. He was part of a great group that included Ally McCoist, Ian Durrant, Owen Coyle, Andy Milne and Craig Brewster. "André completed his Pro Licence in 2008 and the following year I asked him to come back and give a presentation to the new students," admits Fleeting. "I still use his work (a tactical analysis of a match between Scotland and Georgia) as an example to present to my students."

Back in Portugal, with yet another helping hand from Bobby Robson, he joined the youth team's coaching staff at FC Porto. André already felt that he was capable of taking his seat on the bench, as head coach of the youth team. He showed a love of challenges and a total lack of fear. But the Porto structure thought it premature to hand the position of head coach, albeit of the youth team, to a "kid" not much older than 20.

A CARIBBEAN ADVENTURE

Ambitious, daring, reckless. These are the personality traits that led a young, 22 year-old André to reply to a newspaper advert: "Seeking a professional to head the youth team of the British Virgin Islands Football Association (BVIFA)". It does not get any more remarkable than this. "He sent us his CV and, coming from a great club like FC Porto and being a friend of Bobby Robson, we were convinced," says Kenrick Grant, who ran the BVIFA at the time.

While most of his schoolmates were opting for university degrees, André got the job and set off for the tiny country with its 25,000 inhabitants living in an area of little more than 150 square kilometres. He was there for only five months – from December 1999 to April 2000 – and never revealed his age to those in charge at the association. He only did so on his last day: "The Association only discovered he was 22 when he left," admits Grant.

It was all pineapples and paradise beaches – everything a young man could dream of. And at the beginning, he even needed sun block. "When he first arrived he was always on the beach, as if he were on holiday! But when he started to work, he surprised me. He drew up a plan for all the teams, from the youngest to the oldest, including a manual with tactics, and everything was computerised," recalls Grant.

Nevertheless, the stage once more proved to be too small for so much ambition. The experience also earned him the biggest defeat of his career – a 14-1 thrashing inflicted on his team by Bermuda.

"He wasn't impressed with the quality of our players and wanted to go to a great club," reveals Kenrick Grant.

The Caribbean experience was a short-lived one, but one in which Villas-Boas had stepped out of his comfort zone, a trade mark that has featured throughout his career.

A MODEST FOOTBALLER

We have yet to look at André Villas-Boas, the footballer. It would be strange for a boy who felt so passionately about football not to have taken a stab at that dream shared by so many teenage boys: to be a professional football player. Villas-Boas did indeed try, but unsuccessfully.

It was the early 1990s and a group of students from the Colégio do Rosário – including André – decided to form a junior football team to represent Ramaldense, a modest club in Porto which produced, for example, Humberto Coelho, one of the best Portuguese central defenders ever, who went on to shine as a Benfica player.

Strangely enough, André Villas-Boas's footballing career began in goal. At 15, he had arrived at Ramaldense fresh from Ribeirense, a club where he had been a goalkeeper. However, he was not very good, and consequently he had only been selected for three or four games. When he moved to Ramaldense he insisted on playing in goal for a season. Once again he wasn't very successful in this position, and Magalhães switched him to midfield. Nevertheless, during training, Villas-Boas was always keen to go back in goal whenever he could.

As a midfield player, the current Chelsea manager is said to have shown good technique; he defended aggressively and passed well, even though the pitch they played on had a poor surface. Joaquim Magalhães, the club's coach at the time, put André in the first team, which was fighting against relegation in Porto's city league. "He was reserved and very polite," says the coach, "although he was already giving orders to his mates on the pitch. You could see he was a leader."

In André's short career as a player, Ramaldense was followed by Marechal Gomes da Costa (MGC). An amateur team, it was made up of engineers, doctors and students, all from affluent backgrounds. It was an exciting season at the club (whose motto, "You'll never drink alone", was a rather obvious pun on the Liverpool motto), as they had only just joined the amateur league. As there was nowhere else available, it was run from coach Manuel Ribeiro's car, which transported everything to do with the club.

Manuel Ribeiro remembers a "cheerful young man, with a great sense of humour". On the pitch he was "a fighter" and would already direct his colleagues "using what he'd learnt as assistant coach of FC Porto's youth team." Only one thing would wipe the smile off his face – defeat. "He didn't take well to bad results. He'd be upset and downcast," says Manuel Ribeiro.

Pedro Barros, captain of the MGC club at the time, had met André when both played squash at the English Club, and both of them were at MGC in 1998. Pedro recalls that "André was a strong player, who was fearless and had great stamina." However, André had an increasing workload with Porto's youth team, and a lack of time was the decisive factor that led him to quit MGC at the end of the 1998-99 season. MGC played on Saturdays and as Pedro Barros explains, as his career progressed Villas-Boas could no longer have Saturdays off.

2

THE EYES AND EARS
OF MOURINHO

*"For me, André is a key element. He deserves all
the money they pay him!"*

José Mourinho[10]

Probably looking more tanned, but certainly wanting to take on more stimulating challenges, André Villas-Boas left the Caribbean and came back home to FC Porto. He once again took up his post with the youth team, working directly with Ilídio Vale, who ran the Porto Academy at the time and is currently the national coach for Portugal's Under-20 team.

Villas-Boas's return coincided with the arrival of José Mourinho, who was replacing Octávio Machado as manager. At the time, FC Porto were occupying a modest 5th place in the League, and were consequently in danger of not qualifying for either of the UEFA competitions. Their defeat by Boavista (2-0), on the 19th match day, had forced president Pinto da Costa[11] to take a rare decision. He fired Machado, and very quickly signed José Mourinho, whose quality of work at União de Leira had not gone unnoticed.

Mourinho brought along his assistants, Rui Faria and Baltemar Brito from Leiria. And he chose former international player, Silvino

---

10. *"Mourinho: Porquê Tantas Vitórias?" (Mourinho: Why So Many Victories?), (Gradiva, February 2006).*
11. *Jorge Nuno Pinto da Costa has been president of FC Porto since 1982 and is one of the directors, if not the director, with the most titles in the history of world football. There is an old saying, originally proffered by a coach (Mário Wilson) who came to Benfica in the 70s – "Whoever coaches Benfica runs the risk of being champion" – a saying which nowadays fits FC Porto like a glove.*

Louro, as his goalkeeper coach. However, he was still short of one member of his new coaching staff, someone to observe opposition teams and players. Six years before, during his time at FC Porto as Bobby Robson's assistant, Mourinho had already heard about young André's competency and ambition. Villas-Boas was now 23 years old and completely different to that "merely" inquisitive teen to whom Sir Bobby Robson had given a helping hand.

José Mourinho concluded that the young André Villas-Boas must now surely be stronger and more mature from a technical point of view, given all the studying he had done and the experience he had acquired over the previous six years. Following this line of thinking, he asked Ilídio Vale if he could invite AVB to join the coaching staff he was putting together. Vale agreed. "We knew that he had qualities and that he was ambitious," explains the current Under-20 national coach.

André started working with José Mourinho's coaching staff on a part-time basis through to the end of the 2001-02 season. All that was asked of the new manager who had just arrived from Leiria was to stabilise things that season with the best ranking possible. Winning the League was little more than a fantasy: by the 19th match day, the Dragons were trailing first-placed Sporting by 7 points, and in Portugal – in a League that is not very competitive – it was practically impossible to make up that difference. Yet, under the command of a new coaching team, FC Porto went on to play 15 difficult matches (11 wins, two draws and two defeats), jumping from 5th place to 3rd, moving past Benfica, something which is always cause for celebration among the Dragons.

André Villas-Boas joined José Mourinho's coaching staff full-time at the beginning of the following season, 2002-03, when FC Porto went on to deliver one of the best performances in their history, achieving a treble by winning the Portuguese League, the Portuguese Cup and the UEFA Cup.

Villas-Boas's work proved to be extremely useful, going beyond anything of the sort that had been done before. He left absolutely nothing to chance. He set new standards in terms of the level of detail and the depth of his analyses, and he created what came to be known as "The Opponent Observation Department".

His ability to identify the opposition's most important points in a succinct manner was especially appreciated by Mourinho and the squad. The analyses of how their opponents played were accompanied by personal DVDs for the players, containing an in-depth analysis of a player's direct opponent.

Ricardo Carvalho, who worked with Villas-Boas at FC Porto for two years, and then at Chelsea for three years, has said that "the reports he draws up are extremely thorough. He can scrutinise an opponent right down to the smallest detail. Nothing gets past him. He knows everything about the players and everything about the teams." Paulo Ferreira, who has followed a similar footballing path to Ricardo, confirmed the same thing: "Our preparation before matches is incredible. I go into a match knowing everything about what my opponent does. I had never seen anything like this before."

"QUARTERED" OPPONENTS

As an example, and so as to better understand the quality of his work, let's take a look at the report that André Villas-Boas prepared for the first great European final of José Mourinho's career: the 2003 UEFA Cup Final between FC Porto and Glasgow Celtic held in Seville. Martin O'Neill was manager of Celtic at the time.

There are four A4 pages filled with condensed and well organised information, leaving nothing out, and including 24 pitch schemes showing all the movements and systems used by the Scots and an individual analysis of each opposition player. All of this followed up by numerous suggestions.

DEFENSIVE ORGANISATION

- Team organised in a medium/low block, a lot of pressure with an increase of intensity in the midfield, be it through visual references or through the clustering of players, with the added factor that lines are close together and there is no space between them. They are very rough – fouls!!

- The centre-backs tighten all approaching movements by the forward players towards the holder of the ball. They concede some depth behind them that can be exploited – especially when the centre-backs are dragged out of their space and Balde is left alone. There is also space to exploit behind Agathe and Thompson, forcing the centre-back on that side to compensate, leaving a gap to use. They do not play for offside. They are very strong in the air and dominate first and second ball. Without exception, all centre-backs are slow to rotate/react. Against two forwards, Mjalby and Valgaeren mark with Balde providing cover.

- Midfield triangle well defined, they like to press together, but display 'laziness' when faced with an opponent moving the ball around. It makes them indecisive. In this respect Lennon is the first to give up. He is very strong but only at short range. In situations where Petrov and Sutton are not in position as they have taken off from deep, they are left numerically inferior in the midfield. They have difficulties and the team becomes very 'fragile' and 'breaks up' easily.

- High pressure is dictated by the forwards that pressure our centre-backs when they are in trouble, midfielders also help and for a time seriously curtail the opponents time and space in certain areas. It is very important to stretch the team. They kill the holder of the ball.

- Larsson can drop back to pressure the adversary's defensive midfielder from behind. A lot of aggressiveness and commitment in 50/50 balls. Space behind the full-backs/wingers. They are the ones who pressure our full-backs when they have the ball.

TRANSITION AFTER LOSING THE BALL

- Medium/slow change of attitude, wing backs are fragile, as well as the midfield, which isn't populated. Take a while to recover positions. It is possible to break in a counter attack.

- Strong reaction to the ball, there is no control of space. The closest man is good at exerting pressure but, in general, they are slow on recovery, they have problems with the space behind them and become separated as they don't have their lines close together.

- Unexpected high pressure or following a positive emotional moment in the game. Aggressiveness in individual confrontations. Many fouls.

SET PLAYS AGAINST

- During lateral free kicks they form a two-man wall (which jumps), leave a man in the area and all the others mark man on man. Larsson stays in front.

- During free kicks from in front they form a five-man wall (they jump). They are all very tall and as the player approaches to kick the ball they move closer to it. During indirect free kicks there is always a player breaking from the wall too soon. Warn referee.

- In corner kicks they place a man on each post and one in the zone between the near post and the six-yard box. All the others man mark. They leave Larsson in front to break rapidly for the counter attack.

- A lot of pressure on our throw-ins. Distracted and vulnerable with short corners.

ATTACK ORGANISATION

- A passionate team, going through a good period, they try hard and put a lot into the game. Persistent, aggressive and showing strong self-belief. They organise themselves in a 3-5-2 structure (with a defensive pivot); dynamic, they know how to play short or direct, the game is narrow and feeds off the axis of the two midfielders plus the pivot and the two forwards. They play at different rhythms, with changes of orientation in the direction of the game, with Lennon constantly supporting the rear and the attacking pivot dropping into the open spaces.

- Long throws from the goalkeeper. Very strong in the air. They can try two things: 1) a forward approaches the ball to flick it backwards towards the other moving forward; 2) a forward approaches the ball, holds and kicks it to the midfield triangle (always close and 'sniffing' for the second ball), which he places deep to the lateral midfielders who are as far up as possible.

- The midfielders are very positional. Lennon is fixed. It's a back pass line that guarantees balance. Lambert has more attacking presence, but both provide coverage to allow the wing midfielders to move forward. Pay attention to Lambert, who likes taking off with the ball and playing combinations with the central forwards. Petrov accelerates the game. He dribbles well and in finding spaces he is lethal appearing deftly, always with the right timing. Also lots of combination passes with the forwards.

- The outside midfielders behave normally. In the 2nd phase they are at maximum width. When they receive the ball Agathe likes to search out the centre forward, who runs into space behind our full-back, the one who will pressure him, to then move in and allow a new pass line or, drives the ball in and seeks the furthest player forward, who lays-off the ball to the other central forward who has run into the space in front of him or gone deep. Thompson likes being open at all times and when he receives the ball he engages in a face off with the full-back. The one on one approach is characteristic: leading the ball up to the defence and at the last moment dribbling in or out to cross immediately.

- Hartson has ability in the air; he holds the ball up well and holds it in dangerous areas to play in combination with Larsson. Larsson has positional freedom, drifts to both sides, moves to the wings, drops short and deep. Technically he is very good.

- They are excellent at holding position in the penalty area. One forward is at the near post while the other is around the penalty spot. Then Sutton arrives at the far post, or through the middle, and the winger from the opposite side also arrives at the far post or out of the penalty area.

- Lots of passes from the centre-backs to the forwards (aerial and low), and to Petrov, who immediately spins or releases on first touch to the forward who has already run into space.

TRANSITION AFTER GAINING BALL POSSESSION

- Clearance kicks are the most dangerous.

- Quick change of attitude. Depth is always the first option.

- Larsson anticipates the depth, 'stretches' the opponent and is at the off-side limit, or moves down towards the ball to break in pressing, and rotates to pass or lead.

- Beware of the wingers. Rapid transitions by Agathe who moves in, exchanging positions with the centre forward and knows how to strike from afar. Thompson is left open and crosses on first touch.

- When our full-backs have to exert pressure in the centre the forward is always within a passing line, moving behind – they place the ball there with ease, from near or far.

SET PLAYS FOR

- Free kicks on both sides are taken by Thompson. He can shoot directly or cross. He crosses with extreme quality as five players run in. Incisive movements, attacking the ball.

- A lot of quality and variety in free kicks in front of the goal. Thompson almost always takes them, whether they are short or long. He doesn't have a fixed direction and can shoot to the nearest or to the furthest side from the keeper.

- Corners taken on both sides by Thompson. If Petrov is on the pitch he takes them from the left. Petrov aims corners very close to the goalkeeper. There is a man by the keeper who attacks the ball at the near post if it's a close corner and at the far post if it's an open corner. Positioning varies from corner to corner. Lots of confusion in close corners.

- The second ball is very dangerous.

- Throw-ins in the offensive third of field are long to the penalty box where Hartson appears to head the ball.

OBSERVATIONS

- All fouls in their midfield, they build wide and apply the same building principles starting from the goalkeeper.

- They are implacable when protecting the ball with the body, they open their arms and it's difficult to steal the ball. Beware of Larsson and Maloney's explosive turns.

- Clever simulations of fouls, especially on the edge of the penalty box.

- They can invert the midfield triangle during the game or when they are ahead, playing with Lennon further behind and Lambert and Petrov up front.

- Very dangerous at set plays.

- When they are behind on goals Maloney may come in. Very fast – be careful with depth. He also takes set plays.

- Yellow and red cards – they commit lots of fouls.

INDIVIDUAL ASSESSMENT

- 20 Douglas – Good goalkeeper, tall and good at picking out crosses and punching the ball. Some incomplete saves – always looking for the second ball.

- 35 Malby – Good aerial game, very limited technically. He likes playing deep or searching out Agathe. He squeezes and leaves position when the forward approaches the ball. Aggressive, he commits many fouls.

- 4 McNamara – Good centre-back, he knows how to play and organise the team. Communicative.

- 6 Balde – Very tall and very strong in frontal aerial plays. He has difficulties when faced with an agile and explosive forward. Very weak in one-on-ones as he is unable to spin and chase, so he will always try to intercept or commit a foul. He plays as a sweeper and won't commit off-sides.

- 5 Valgaeren – Likes to leave the defensive third and run with the ball – he takes chances and the ball can be taken from him. Good in the air, slow on turn around.

- 17 Agathe – Very good technically, he plays wide open and in deep. He knows how to combine passes and also to lead on the inside. His positioning in phase 2 and 3 compromises defensive transition (there is a lot of space behind him). Explosive changes of pace.

- 8 Thompson – Good left foot, he places the ball with ease, no matter whether it's with long passes, diagonals, crossing or shooting. In a one-on-one situation he goes straight to the full-back then breaks in or out. Crosses have direction and are dangerous. Important in set plays.

- 18 Lennon – Midfielder with defensive responsibilities. Very strong but only in his area and is responsible for covering midfielders, wingers and centre-backs. When he isn't there the team is very unbalanced. He is attracted to the ball, which means there is space behind. He knows how to pass and is very aggressive.

- 14 Lambert – Midfielder with most freedom. Very good

technically, he can play as support, always moving, but he also likes to leave his position for short passes with the forwards or to take the ball to the attacking third. He is impressive on passes and very comfortable with short, medium and long distances. He sometimes appears in the penalty area from the back and through the middle.

- 19 Petrov – Restless. He is very intelligent in occupying spaces and always moves up well from behind. If the two forwards move to the same side, Petrov immediately appears. Good technically, he likes to run with the ball after receiving a pass. He takes corners and free kicks.

- 9 Sutton – Centre forward best suited to being an attacking pivot. He uses his head well and is essential in positioning himself by the goalkeeper as he is one of the players that tries to flick on to the two forwards. He has some mobility. He isn't strong technically but knows how to play first touch. Lay-off to midfielders. Dangerous in set plays.

- 10 Hartson – Great athletic build, powerful on contact, good heading abilities. He is slow and isn't very mobile, but when the ball reaches his feet he protects it well while waiting for support. Very important in phase 3. Strong and placed shots, mid and long distance.

- 7 Larsson – Very good technically and dominates attacking combinations. He knows how to play first touch but also knows how to hold, cross and shoot. He is very mobile and always moves with a tactical purpose – behind the centre- and full-backs. Fast at short and mid distances. Intelligent.

- 29 Maloney – Forward (like Rui Barros), short but very dangerous. Very fast and with a lot of versatility. He may come into play when they are down on score. Explosive and capable in open confrontations. Jumps well – be careful.

FC Porto won the match in extra time by 3-2, in a final that has not been forgotten by the club's fans due to the enormous expectations preceding it, the fantastic atmosphere surrounding the match and, of course, the incredible emotion of the final victory. An emotion which, as any Porto fan will tell you, was even greater than that felt a year later when the same team won the Champions League.

At a certain stage, a 2005 report on Newcastle drawn up by André Villas-Boas, made its way onto the Internet. It was full of observations, among which we can find the following:

"Team going through an excellent period. Motivated and finally finding its balance. Important to keep focus as they will keep high intensity. | Very quick and alert team to react to attacking 2nd balls – after winning it they have options and excellent transitions | depth directed at Owen. | Very poor defensive transitions after set plays. They leave players in the back to maintain superiority, but cannot deal with the counter-attack into space. This is even more obvious on Babayaro's side – possible to kill. | Substitutions don't imply a change of system of play. But the diamond shape can always be an option. | Players on the bench have a lot of technical quality and can change the game. Kieron Dyer and Lee Bowyer are dynamic and always assume roles that make full use of their mobility. Ameobi is always a threat in the air and in set plays. Luque has technique. Owen chases all lost balls and back-passes to goalkeeper (great danger!)."

However, what is even more interesting, especially now as Villas-Boas has returned to England to head Chelsea, and even taking into account the time that has gone by and the fact that the players are no longer the same – only Giggs remains on the team but is not a regular – is to discover how he scouted Sir Alex Ferguson's Manchester United, who are undoubtedly one of the most difficult opponents that he will face in the Premier League. As always, a systematically organised report, taking into account the opponent's structure both in attack and defence, their attacking movements (after winning the ball) and their defensive movements (after losing the ball), set plays for and against, an individual player analysis, and observations of a general nature. Let's take a look then at some enlightening notes about what he conveyed to José Mourinho.

Villas-Boas considered Manchester United to be a team that was "fast on the offensive, with strong collective organisation and extremely objective in possession of the ball as well as in direct long ball play. High level of individual talent that is always at the service of the team. A strong team spirit and intense pace during the game. Very dynamic, lots of penetrating movements off the ball and very efficient at finishing." He also drew particular attention to the forwards' movements. "Great play in the penalty area. Van Nistelrooy holds it with his back to the goal and combines with the supporting players. Several typically English combinations. The forward's movement is made according to the holder of the ball: on a diagonal, opening a line of passing to receive, or shoot or the decoy movements of approaching the ball to then take off deep. Saha is excellent at organising the game with his back to the goal; he drops to the midfield – freeing his space up for Giggs or Nistelrooy – turns and takes off deep". He went on to say that "positional sense is very strong. Giggs may appear at the near post during crosses from the opposite side. He attacks the ball from the front and gets ahead of the centre-backs. Scholes arrives from behind (very fast – jumps strongly and with a high quality of finishing). Van Nistelrooy never puts himself in a position to be marked. He always places himself behind the centre-back so that he and the ball are never visible at the same time. He normally pretends he is going to the near post then drifts to the far post or vice-versa (or he stays still and attacks the ball by surprise). Saha is in the penalty area".

From a defensive point of view he noted that the central defence was "a little permissive and expectant", especially if the pair was Brown/O'Shea. "When marking their direct opponents they allow themselves to be dragged across to midfield – it's important to drag them out and create a hole, a passive Brown allows his opponent to turn against him." He further observed that "in the defensive third, they rarely apply the offside, and there are situations in which the centre-back is 15/20 metres behind in relation to the full-back – the ball can go in between positions." Another vulnerability Villas-Boas detected had to do with the defensive positioning of the two centre midfielders, Scholes and Keane. "They are always well placed, but if Scholes doesn't recover position after losing the ball, Keane is left alone in the whole space. During the opposite side's penetration movements, there are times when they let themselves be dragged into a one-on-one situation." If the opponent took off with a long ball the whole team would concentrate midfield "within 30 metres", thus leaving "space in depth" that could be "taken advantage of with a strong kick".

When Manchester United lost the ball, André Villas-Boas noticed a "rapid change of attitude" with "high and 'suffocating' pressure in the first phase of their opponent's attacking movement." The team would tighten the lines because the midfielders took chances, "shortening up to the half-way line", and opening "spaces in deep but placing players off-side." For this scout on Mourinho's technical team at Chelsea, the centre midfielders exerted "strong pressure near the sidelines", causing "the opponent a serious reduction in space and time", but leaving the "central area open".

In attacking movements, he believed there was significant danger if Chelsea lost the ball in their own midfield. He also highlighted the "pace of the ball, greater speed in player's movements, and a lot of depth from attackers and also from midfielders. Rapid options with crosses and players coming forward from back to front in the attacking third." For André Villas-Boas, Giggs and Nistelrooy were key players because they had "strong individual transitions". Giggs performed "movements behind our full-back to receive", while Nistelrooy either came "from between the lines to receive and proceed", or he wanted "immediate depth to stretch the opponent", even if he didn't receive the ball.

Another dangerous situation he drew attention to had to do with the fact that "every foul in the midfield" was "immediately taken. They are fouled, get up and quickly resume playing", taking off from "the exposed side of the opponent". On the other hand, he also pointed out the "immense pressure on our keeper with the second ball", in which case it would be important to protect him in that type of situation. The free kicks from the side were taken by Giggs or Scholes "right towards the goal, to the diagonal run of five players", with Keane at the edge of the area "to control the second ball". He also explained that corners always took "the ball close to the goal", with "diagonal and explosive" moves.

All this was illustrated with attractive colour schemes, showing the area of the pitch being referred to and the movements of the opposing players, appropriately "kitted out" in red.

In André Villas-Boas' opinion, Manchester displayed "a lot of passivity in defensive marking" of an opponent's set plays, especially Brown and O'Shea. In the majority of these situations the team would choose man-to-man marking, almost always leaving Nistelrooy up front and Giggs in the midfield. "They have a very strong transition after winning back the ball – they connect through Giggs or through any one of the players that leaves the penalty area and runs with the ball."

Curiously, at the time André Villas-Boas didn't consider Cristiano Ronaldo a major cause for concern. The Portuguese winger is hardly referred to throughout the report, other than in the competent scout's individual assessments, where he observes that Ronaldo would gather the ball in position and then go "on top of the left full-back in a one-on-one", drawing attention to the fact that he was "very fast and explosive". He also noted that he "dribbled and controlled the ball" and that he easily eliminated an opponent's "blind" pressure.

Apart from this, the extremely detailed individual assessments confirmed what had already been said about the team's attacking and defensive movements. For example, amongst many other observations, he thought Keane had a "fast pace throughout the whole game", was "very strong positionally" and that he contested "the face offs for the ball with extreme aggression". Scholes, with dynamic football, was a "key player at every stage of the game", he had "an incredible pass, no matter whether short, long or penetrating" and a "very dangerous mid-distance shot". Fletcher "seems slow but has a long stride, looks like a bungler but is coordinated and executes rapidly", besides which, being a short pass player, he "always gave continuity", he never left the "ball to chance". Huge compliments for Ryan Giggs – "fantastic player on the outside or the inside" – about whom he wrote "if he lodges himself on the wing, he attacks the right full-back" to cross or to shoot, or "he can come looking for the inside space, taking on the movement of the game to the attacking third, combining with the strikers as he moves forward". He considered him "dangerous in the shift to attack" for he could "move from defence to attack with ease". Van Nistelrooy was another highly appreciated player, about whom he wrote several lines, and thought him to be an "amazing goal scorer", that "was never capable of being marked" and that he dominated the off-side, positioning himself "behind our defensive line", and then "with circular or diagonal movements" getting himself back into an on-side position. Saha, despite not being tall, had "an incredible jump" and liked to "drop to the midfield to help his colleagues and relieve pressure".

The less positive observations were left for two players from United's back line. John O'Shea was seen as being a "heavy, and a little static, centre or full-back defender", and, notwithstanding having good timing with his tackles, he wasn't a fast player and had "difficulties turning round", being "clumsy with or without the ball". Wes Brown, in spite of being tall and good positionally, made many mistakes and was "very passive, especially with set plays". He considered goalkeeper, Tim Howard to be "brave, very agile and communicative", with "complete saves" and good at turning defence into attack; Gary Neville was "effective in tackles" and, having recovered his space properly, would not stop playing "hard", being "easily" irritated and making "excellent crosses", while his brother, Phil Neville, was a versatile player who performed positionally and was "very effective in marking", but had a "limited view of the game".

Through these examples one can observe the detail and care that André Villas-Boas took in observing his opponents – to analyse them in depth he needed to observe for four to five matches in order to understand if things happened randomly or if, on the contrary, they were the result of standard movements – and thereafter in compiling the data that helped Mourinho to prepare the team for so many and such significant victories. But one shouldn't overstate his contribution too much, valuable as it may have been – and it was! After all, during the 2009/10 season in which André Villas-Boas "abandoned" Mourinho, the Special One achieved an absolutely "impossible" treble whilst working with Inter: winning the Serie A League Title, the Coppa Italia and the Champions League!

007 – MISSION "UNITED"

His reports, however, were not limited to a thorough description of an opponent's style of play. Villas-Boas would also go to the opposition's training grounds, in disguise, in order to get an idea of the state of mind amongst players, the team atmosphere and the most frequently used moves. Then he would put together DVDs with images from the game, giving emphasis to set plays, attacking and defensive movements, etc. All of this was ten years ago.

With astuteness and, it must be said, under the supervision of José Mourinho, Villas-Boas inaugurated a new chapter in scouting: to the point that Mourinho would later say that André was his "eyes and ears".

The two worked together for close on seven years, and while it is true that at the beginning Mourinho "invented" Villas-Boas, later it was Villas-Boas who knew how to "reinvent himself", by constantly adding value to what he did.

Early on, José Mourinho had become aware of the importance of a scouting department for a top coaching set-up. He realised this as soon as he began preparing his first match as head coach at Benfica. Their opponents had been Boavista and, as always, the club had sent one of its scouts to draw up a report. In his notes, the observer forgot to mention Erwin Sanchez – "only" the most influential player on the team. Faced with such a serious oversight, Mourinho decided that from then on this responsibility would always fall on his coaching staff, and be under his direction. This was also something that the Portuguese coach was already very familiar with, as a result of his work as Louis van Gaal's assistant coach at Barcelona. At Benfica, he paid, out of his own pocket, for an external collaborator, in whom he placed his trust, to scout their opponents. After receiving the information, Mourinho would himself scrutinise it and prepare a summary for the players. He would then present it in the dressing room on a huge flipchart.

During his time at Benfica and União de Leiria, in the first two years of his career as a manager, José Mourinho didn't have anybody working on a permanent basis in the scouting department. Stability and sustained development only came about in 2002 at FC Porto, when André Villa-Boas joined the coaching staff. The club already had a scouting department, which was in fact efficient, but Mourinho – via Villas-Boas – revolutionised it: he radically changed the way to scout opponents, systematise information and present the findings. The changes were reflected in the results on the pitch.

After the remarkable work carried out at FC Porto – which culminated in winning two Portuguese Leagues, a Portuguese Cup, a Portuguese Super Cup, a UEFA Cup and the Champions League – the footballing world had many questions about how José Mourinho's method would work out at Chelsea. This scrutiny also extended to those working with him. Would the methods used so successfully in Portugal, a country where football is not as competitive, work in England – the country of the footballing vanguard?

As far as scouting was concerned, there was a total surprise! The work planned by José Mourinho and carried out by André Villas-Boas was miles ahead of anything being done in the Premier League. And the Portuguese made a point of showing this as soon as they began preparations for their first season, 2004-05. As it happened, Chelsea and Manchester United both went on a pre-season trip to the United States. By that time, everyone knew that the luck of the draw meant a match between the two clubs, on the very first day of the Premiership.

Mourinho was perfectly aware that to be successful in England, they first had to break down the compulsive domination of Alex Ferguson's team. Mourinho also knew that a victory over their arch rivals, right at the beginning of the championship, would represent a huge psychological advantage. He wasted no time. He asked André Villas-Boas to embark on a veritable 007 mission. An impossible mission: to observe closely all the steps taken by the Red Devils in the United States. Training sessions, states of mind, injuries, moods... everything found its way into Villas-Boas's notepad. It was a remarkable job, worthy of an entry in any compendium on the scouting of opponents.

The most visible result of this strategy was the game itself, held at Stamford Bridge on 14 August 2004. Chelsea won 1-0 (Gudjohnsen, 15'), in 90 minutes that had been planned in detail. It is not possible to quantify the impact this result had on Chelsea winning the 2004-05 Premier League, but one thing is certain: that afternoon the Blues planted their first flag in a territory previously dominated by Manchester United .

In an interview he gave shortly after joining Chelsea as part of Mourinho's coaching staff, Villas-Boas admitted that he found ways of secretly watching the training sessions of his club's opponents so as to be able to obtain "illicit" information. "My work enables José to know exactly when a player from the opposition team is likely to be at his best or his weakest. I travel to watch practices, often incognito, and look at our opponents' physical and mental state before drawing my conclusions."

José Mourinho's methods, and particularly the importance given to scouting opponents, took the directors at Chelsea by surprise. Neither the club, nor the English were used to this type of work. Brian McDermott, Reading manager, often ran into Villas-Boas when scouting throughout the country. He says he learnt a great deal from André and remembers seeing him compile reports on his Blackberry. "Now he is a fearless manager. He speaks English very well; he is friendly and the kind of coach who always speaks about the players, seeing them as more important than himself. This convinces players," confirms McDermott.

IN THE EYE OF THE HURRICANE

Mourinho's teams – those that go out onto the pitch to play, but also the coaching staff that support him – are known for their visible team spirit and for the intense struggle they are willing to undertake in order to achieve common objectives. There are no half measures: you're either on board or you're not.

In February 2005, when Chelsea visited the Nou Camp for the final sixteen of the Champions League, Mourinho had already had a few run-ins with UEFA. At half-time, Chelsea were leading 1-0, but in the second half, after Didier Drogba was sent off (on 56 minutes), Barcelona turned things around and ended up winning 2-1 (goals on 67 and 73 minutes). At the end, Mourinho accused Barcelona's manager, Frank Rijkaard, of having been in referee Anders Frisks's dressing room, and said that, consequently, he was not at all surprised by what he viewed as the decisive sending-off of Didier Drogba in the second half of the match. At that time, Mourinho was a contributor to the now extinct weekly magazine *Dez* which came with the sports newspaper *Record*. He wrote in his column, "I couldn't believe it when I saw Rijkaard walk into the referee's dressing room."

Mourinho's accusations didn't go down at all well in many sectors of the football world and unleashed numerous reactions from referee organisations (who even contemplated going on strike), as well as from UEFA and from FIFA itself. But, worst still was that this situation led the Swedish referee, one of the most highly esteemed in Europe, to end a most successful career at the highest level. Frisk abandoned football because, as he said, he feared for the safety of his family after having received various death threats for allegedly making it easier for Barcelona to beat Chelsea.

This, however, is not the strangest part of the story. At that time, André Villas-Boas was already known as being one of José Mourinho's most volatile collaborators, and perhaps even more controversial than the boss himself – and it has been said that it was him, and not Mourinho, that had claimed to have seen Rijkaard go into Anders Frisk's dressing room three times during half-time. All of which makes perfect sense, as it would have been quite natural for Mourinho to be in the dressing room at half-time, giving instructions to his team. Shortly afterwards, Mourinho himself admitted this: "Rijkaard met with the referee in his dressing room for over five minutes. I know this because my assistants were standing at the door during the meeting."

In the second leg, at Stamford Bridge, Chelsea won 4-2 and made it through to the next round. It was a memorable game, which Chelsea later sold on DVD by the thousands. Mourinho was suspended by UEFA as a result of the Nou Camp incident and was not able to lead the Blues from the bench for the two quarter-final matches against Bayern Munich, who were nevertheless eliminated by Chelsea. In addition, he was also fined by UEFA – as were Chelsea.

THE ON-DUTY COMMENTATOR

At the end of the second season at Chelsea (2005-06) – which once again earned Mourinho's coaching staff more medals as the club won the Premier League and the FA Community Shield – the football world turned its attentions to the World Cup in Germany.

At around this time, the Spanish newspaper *Marca* published an in depth report detailing the way in which the coaching staff headed by José Mourinho worked. Among the various elements mentioned in the article, the work carried out by the scout André Villas-Boas stood out. The thoroughness, the detail, the wealth of information and the use of new technology caught the attention of the directors of SIC, one of the four terrestrial TV channels in Portugal.

SIC had acquired the rights to broadcast the 2006 World Cup, and were looking for capable professionals to add to their studio commentary team. After the article in *Marca*, the channel had their eye on André Villas-Boas. Illustrious yet unknown, he lived away from the spotlight – almost always travelling around the world or locked away in offices writing up reports. He wasn't even a regular presence at Chelsea training sessions. He also had no experience of television commentary. He did, however, have enormous potential to offer a competent and, above all, rather different approach – unlike anything that had been done on Portuguese TV previously.

André Villas-Boas was receptive and enthusiastic from the very start and the channel decided to hire him. Always ambitious and willing to try something different, the job offered a precious window of opportunity. It brought the possibility of giving visibility to a job that is by definition "invisible". As Villas-Boas himself admitted in 2005, in an interview for Chelsea TV, the video of which was widely viewed on the Internet, "I spend most of my time at the computer drawing up reports for this man (José Mourinho). And for him to be satisfied, I have to do them as well as possible."

As head of the coaching staff, the final say on Villas-Boas's venture at SIC was down to José Mourinho. The Portuguese coach had never been very keen on drawing attention to his collaborators. Furthermore, he also wanted the secret workings of his coaching staff to remain within the four walls of his office. However, he himself had appeared on television – admittedly not often – as a commentator with vast coaching experience (on SportTV, the only Portuguese channel exclusively dedicated to sport). Also, the offer made to Villas-Boas would take place during the close season, right in the middle of the holidays and outside the working period at Chelsea. With few real reasons to say no, Mourinho agreed.

And so, for the first time, Villas-Boas appeared publicly, commentating in studio before and after Portugal's matches in the 2006 World Cup. He was clear, concise, informed, insightful and – no less important – he had a captivating television image. He surprised everyone. However, what really set his commentaries apart was his use of a tablet to explain, via the touch-screen system, the tactical moves of the teams. An absolute innovation on Portuguese television and a total break from what had been done before then.

The staff at SIC were highly impressed with Villas-Boas's work:

"He would ask us to freeze apparently trivial images, with no interesting details, but once he explained them, they would make complete sense. He saw things that no one else saw."

André Villas-Boas's television success apparently bothered José Mourinho. Whether as a result of it or not, Mourinho also accepted an offer from SIC – something he'd previously always turned down – to commentate in studio on the World Cup quarter-final match between England and Portugal (1-3 after a penalty shoot-out).

After his stint at SIC, Villas-Boas returned to anonymity... until November 2007. Two months earlier, on 20 September 2007, José Mourinho's coaching staff and Chelsea had come to an agreement regarding the termination of their contract, bringing to an end a 3-year relationship. Though nominally still a member of Mourinho's staff, Villas-Boas was effectively unemployed. He wasted little time and within two months had accepted an offer to commentate on SportTV, having once again secured the necessary approval from José Mourinho.

Villas-Boas's relationship with SportTV lasted five months, until April 2008. During this time he commentated on ten matches from Portuguese, English and Italian football as well as the Champions League. Oddly enough, both his first and last commentaries were of FC Porto matches, the club most dear to his heart, and where he would shine three years later. No less of a coincidence was that his penultimate commentary was of a match between Lazio and Inter Milan in the Serie A of the Italian League. Thirty-six days later, on 2 June, José Mourinho's coaching staff – of which Villas-Boas was still a part – signed for Inter Milan.

It was around this time that friction between André and José Mourinho began to surface. Villas-Boas was clearly the most resistant of Mourinho's assistants, and the one who continually sought other challenges outside of the coaching staff. Something that the other members – Rui Faria, Silvino and Baltemar Brito – would not even dare think about, much less ask for authorisation to do. The relationship between Mourinho and Villas-Boas was headed down the road of no return. It was the beginning of the end.

THE BREAK AWAY FROM MOURINHO

April 2009. André Villas-Boas had now been working as a member of José Mourinho's coaching team for close on seven years. He had completed another coaching course with the Scottish Football Association. Those who know him and his recent journey understand why he had other ambitions besides scouting opponents and producing invaluable computerised reports. As Helen Keller [12] said: "Why are we content to live on all fours, when we want to fly?"

André Villas-Boas approached Mourinho and spoke to him of his aspirations: he wanted to be closer to the squad, be on the bench and, above all, do field work out on the pitch. Rumour has it that Mourinho replied along the following lines: "You want to do field work? Great... then go and farm. I'm the one in charge here." And then he advised André not to forget his hoe.

The young scout was part of the small nucleus of collaborators José Mourinho had taken with him from Porto to Chelsea, and then later to Inter Milan. The others were Rui Faria – considered to be Mourinho's true right-hand man, the only person the Special One will really not go without, and who has turned down coaching offers from various clubs – and Silvino Louro – the able goalkeeping coach, faithful friend and, as both of them live in Setúbal, frequent travelling companion. Baltemar Brito had also gone from FC Porto to Chelsea, but he didn't move on to Inter Milan. Rui Faria and Silvino Louro later moved to Real Madrid and are part of Real's current coaching staff.

---

12. *Deaf and blind from early childhood, Helen Keller (1880-1968) was an American writer, public speaker and social activist.*

It is said that Mourinho, a believer in dialogue, but an absolute decision-maker, didn't forgive André Villa-Boas for his "boldness" and that from that moment on the young scout's days on Mourinho's staff were numbered. The immediate signing of another Portuguese, José Morais, to do the same type of work, would seem to confirm this.

Mourinho never particularly appreciated his assistant's desire to play a more leading role. The first time this happened, as we saw, was when André Villas-Boas accepted television channel SIC's offer to be a commentator for the 2006 Germany World Cup. Various other incidents followed, and the aspirations Villas-Boas voiced in April 2009 were the final straw.

For Luís Freitas Lobo [13], André Villas-Boas "was the man, the only one on the face of the Earth, to challenge Mourinho, who was angry and furious when André told him haughtily that he wanted to leave Inter because he felt he was a coach and not a mere scout as Mourinho wanted him to be."

There are, however, those close to Real Madrid's coach who say that his "letting go" of Villas-Boas was merely because Mourinho thought there were better options for that type of scouting work. According to this version, Villas-Boas's strong point was not his above-average capacity to scout teams and players, but instead his proficient use of computers and new technology. He had spent almost seven years without being allowed to step onto the pitch and train, confined to scouting trips and offices. At the coaching level he had never been Mourinho's assistant.

We should, however, remember that during that time he had the opportunity to assimilate a great deal of knowledge, given that his job was to process all manner of information and then computerise

---

13. Luís Freitas Lobo, is one of the most highly regarded football analysts in Portugal, and is a regular contributor to some of the most important Portuguese media, such as RTP (television), TSF (radio), Expresso (a weekly newspaper) and A Bola (a daily sports newspaper). He is known to have a close relationship with André Villas-Boas, who presented his book "Planeta do Futebol" when he still worked with José Mourinho.

it. He therefore had access to training plans, exercise schemes, ways to prepare the squad in relation to their opponents, etc. A veritable hands-on course taken with the man that many consider to be the best coach in the world, and who strives for innovation and creativity in his working methods.

André Villas-Boas, who had a contract at Inter for a further three years, didn't accept the marching orders that he'd been given and, with nothing to do, he stayed on at Inter on a veritable "golden shelf" during the end of the 2008-09 season – the season in which Inter won the Italian League – and the beginning of the next season. Then finally in October 2009, he and the Italian club reached an agreement to end his contract. He received the equivalent of a year's salary.

Unlike everything else that happens or relates to José Mourinho, this incident passed by the Portuguese media almost completely unnoticed and they made practically no reference to it at all. Perhaps this is understandable given that Villas-Boas had always been an 'invisible' character on Mourinho's coaching staff. This was publicly confirmed by André himself when in response to a question about José Mourinho leaving Chelsea, explained: "At the time, I was only a part of a very successful machine created by Mourinho. I wasn't involved in the decision. I saw everything from a great distance."

Although he considers the scouting of teams and players to be an essential element in modern football, André Villas-Boas feels that while this work can make a difference, nobody knows to what extent it is a decisive factor in matches. Sometimes it is, sometimes it isn't. Here is yet another reason why he wanted to make the leap, why he wanted to test himself. He felt he had more to offer and he wanted to start coaching. If he could have worked more closely with Mourinho, all the better, but he naturally accepted that the boss did not feel the same.

3

FINALLY... A DOOR OPENS

*"I had rather be first in a village
than second in Rome."*

Julius Caesar

From April to October 2009, while he sat waiting on that "golden shelf" in Milan, Villas-Boas found the door to some clubs shut firmly in his face. One of these clubs, it is said, was Sporting de Braga, with whom everything had apparently been more or less agreed, when out of the blue, he was overtaken at the finishing line by Domingos Paciência. The truth is that the young scout believed strongly in his future as a coach, and even confided to those close to him (as reported by Luís Freitas Lobo in his weekly column in *Expresso*) "these guys don't know that one of these days they'll be talking to the coach of FC Porto!"

Coimbra, in the centre of Portugal, is home to one of the friendliest clubs in Portuguese football – Académica de Coimbra. After years of success, during which their training school produced some of the best Portuguese players, they spent many seasons on a rollercoaster ride between first and second divisions, remaining in the second division for a number of seasons before settling back into the first division in 2002-03. They achieved their best positions in the League in 1966-67 (2nd place) and in 1968-69 (4th place). Their only official title on record was in 1939, when they won the first-ever Portuguese Cup. They were also finalists in the same competition in 1951, 1967 and 1969.

At around that time (October 2009), Académica were rock bottom of the League. With the manager Domingos Paciência having left at the end of the 2008-09 season for Sporting de Braga, president José Eduardo Simões [14] had hired an "old school" coach – Rogério Gonçalves. But the football they were playing wasn't helping them to meet the target set by the club, which was to keep them in the First Division. Results were poor – 3 points from 7 games, 3 draws and 4 defeats, 5 goals scored and 11 conceded.

The atmosphere, therefore, was not the best, and the discontent among the supporters was growing, even finding its way to the ears of the club's president who had to put up with various insults at the end of a home defeat (2-4) against Marítimo.

A habit that is very much a characteristic of Portuguese football is to change coaches, even early on in the season, if things are not going as planned. And so, José Eduardo Simões decided upon the traditional "psychological whipping", and fired Rogério Gonçalves. He then set off in search of a coach with a profile similar to Domingos Paciência – who had previously achieved excellent results at the club. In other words, he was looking for a young, ambitious coach with a modern vision of football.

The president of Académica did not know André Villas-Boas personally. However, they had a mutual friend who often spoke to José Eduardo Simões about Mourinho's young scout – and he had nothing but extremely good things to say about him. Consequently, Villas-Boas was not totally unknown to Simões. In addition to his qualities, "he knew that (André) was someone with a different way of approaching things, that he was available and anxious to kick off his career," explains the president of Académica.

They had already tried to meet up in the past, but scheduling difficulties had made it impossible to do so. This time, however,

14. *José Eduardo Simões is president of the Académica de Coimbra Association. He has the habit of "gambling" on young coaches (sometimes without any experience) from the FC Porto "school", of which good examples are Domingos Paciência, André Villas-Boas, Jorge Costa, José Guilherme and, more recently, Pedro Emanuel. The comments in this book were taken from an interview he gave to BBC Sport as well as from an interview he granted exclusively for this book.*

José Eduardo Simões was determined to "snap up" André Villas-Boas and asked him to visit him in Coimbra. André flew from Milan to Porto, drove to Coimbra, and met up with the Académica president at the latter's home. In less than two hours, José Eduardo Simões was able to assess not only Villas-Boas's character, but also his technical competency, especially in the particularly detailed way that the former scout analysed Académica's team. He was thoroughly convinced. "He brought with him a structured project, based on a very well thought out strategy and very well defined objectives." He spoke of the team's strengths and weaknesses, and what needed doing in order to improve its performance and results. He further impressed Simões with the assertive and professional manner in which he presented the game plans he wanted to implement and the confidence he showed regarding the club's and his own success. And José Eduardo Simões concluded: "He was clearly knowledgeable about the club and the squad, you could see he'd done his homework, a lot of work, it wasn't the sort of document that you could put together hurriedly during a flight..."

His attitude was very much the same as that of José Mourinho, who, in his first meeting with Chelsea's directors, presented them with an entire dossier detailing what he thought of the club and what his aspirations were, thereby completely winning them over and setting the Swede Sven-Goran Ericksson – with whom he was supposedly competing – at a clear and immediate disadvantage.

In terms of the salary that the young coach would be earning, Académica's president says they came to an agreement "very easily", given that both parties were primarily interested in moving ahead quickly.

After having met André Villas-Boas personally, José Eduardo Simões was so convinced that he felt no need to obtain any further information from others who knew the young coach well, namely José Mourinho. He was absolutely sure about the "gamble" that he had taken.

And so, André Villas-Boas, without any previous management experience, but with excellent references and the advantage of having worked on Mourinho's coaching staff for several years, was quickly signed and immediately presented as the manager of Académica de Coimbra on 13 October 2009.

Finally, that very first door had opened for him.

In reality it was a risky step for the former scout to take, the first of many risky steps in a career that is short, but has already been marked by an unparalleled capacity to take on difficult challenges. "At 31 I gave up a comfortable position as a scout at Inter, an incredible salary and a contract that would run for another three years, for Académica who were bottom of the Portuguese League. Nevertheless, I felt good about what I did," he later admitted.

At his official presentation to the press, he recognised a debt of gratitude to Mourinho – "I have to thank him for the opportunity he gave me" – and gave a speech that revealed a strong personality and an ambitious spirit. He had signed on until June 2011, but he planned on staying longer – however long it took to launch his career in earnest.

"TACTICAL PERIODISATION"

The new manager was immediately and happily accepted by everyone at Académica. "Despite his youth and his inexperience, he was welcomed by all, and immediately generated very positive expectations," says José Eduardo Simões. So impressed was he, that the president took a bet with himself as to how long it would take Villas-Boas to also win over everyone in the working group that he was to lead.

The only point of reference that the players had about André Villas-Boas was the same as everyone else's: the work he'd carried out as part of Mourinho's coaching staff. A fact that nonetheless created some optimism among the group. However, when "he arrived at the Academy's auditorium to meet the squad for the very first time, with a powerpoint presentation in which he explained his way of working, his objectives for the Académica project, and what he truly sought to achieve, what the players heard was a strong and clear presentation, not at all repetitive, and one that was easy to take in," a former Académica player told us. What José Eduardo Simões had expected came true. "He didn't take even half an hour to win over the entire squad," confided the president.

The players were extremely pleased with the first training sessions, and found huge differences between Villas-Boas and his predecessor, namely the importance placed on ball possession, the great variety of exercises – closely linked to match situations – and the intensity and fast pace of practices, which were now shorter. Very similar to what José Mourinho does, it should be noted.

Like the Real Madrid coach, André follows the principles of what is known as "tactical periodisation", a method which has been at the root of the success of a new generation of Portuguese coaches and whose principal mentor was (and is) Vítor Frade [15]. Mourinho and Villas-Boas never attended Vítor Frade's lectures at the University of Porto, but Rui Faria, Mourinho's principal assistant, was one of his brightest students, and the "master" still contacts him regularly. Nevertheless, Mourinho had the opportunity to get to know Vítor Frade well when both were on Bobby Robson's coaching staff at FC Porto. He admires him greatly – so much so that he has dedicated some of his most significant victories to him.

In the traditional system, physical, technical, tactical and

---

15. *Vítor Frade, the creator of "tactical periodisation", is a former lecturer at Porto University's Sports Faculty, whose students were some of the most successful Portuguese coaches. Connected to FC Porto for many years, where he worked directly with various coaches, as part of the coaching staff or by merely collaborating with them, he now spends most of his time at Olival, the club's training ground, where he coordinates the entire training area. Down-to-earth and very friendly, he shuns the limelight, and is the greatest reference for everyone working in modern football coaching in Portugal.*

psychological aspects are practised in individual training sessions or, at best, in physical and technical or technical and tactical sessions. In "tactical periodisation", however, the training session must encompass these four components simultaneously and inseparably. Mourinho confirms this absolutely when he states: "I do not do physical work. I defend the globalisation of the work. I do not know where the physical begins, and the psychological and tactical end." And in 2004, Villas-Boas commented on exactly that: "Some coaches prefer to concentrate more on fitness or mental strength, but José likes to marry together all aspects of training."

In "tactical periodisation" all the training sessions are carried out with a ball, so that the player thinks constantly about the game. Emphasis is therefore given to sessions based on match situations, with the physical component included in these exercises. This is why it is commonly said – and Mourinho himself admits it, as we saw above – there is no so-called fitness trainer on Mourinho's coaching staff, an essential member of the conventional technical teams. This concept is beautifully explained in a remark made by Professor Manuel Sérgio [16]: "In order to learn how to play the piano, the pianist doesn't run around it, he simply plays the piano!"

The most important aspects of "tactical periodisation" can be set out as follows:

- The tactical component commands the entire training process. The other components (physical, technical and psychological) should arise in relation to the demands of the match model adopted by the coach.

---

16. *Manuel Sérgio was one of the first authors, on a worldwide level, to view football (and sports in general) as a social and human science and, as such, to emphasis the principle of complexity as the methodology necessary to comprehend the practice of sport. The fact that he is a philosopher, prevented many coaches from understanding the core of his message. But this did not prevent José Mourinho, who took his subject "Philosophy of Corporal Activities", from adopting his principles.*

- The work is carried out at high levels of intensity.

- The volume (time of execution) never impairs the intensity (speed of execution) of the exercises.

- The exercises are created to mirror match situations.

- The exercises must be motivating and enjoyable, always maintaining a competitive spirit so as to promote the concentration levels of players.

- Being fit means complying with the demands of the game plan adopted, and not only being well physically.

- The weekly tactical plan is drawn up in relation to the next opponent.

It should be noted, however, that this training methodology demands a great deal of imagination from the coach, especially as he has constantly to create exercises, both in terms of quantity (so as not to tire the players) and in terms of quality (so that the practice is carried out as much as possible in relation to the upcoming opponent); exercises which, as we have seen, encompass the four aspects of training.

In addition to the training sessions, however, the players at Académica were also impressed by the new manager's dedication to his work. Villas-Boas arrived at the club's training ground at eight in the morning, and would only leave at between seven and eight in the evening. Knowing that he only held one daily training session, usually at around ten in the morning; it was clear that he spent a great many hours in his day taking care of and preparing everything related to the team. "When I had to make my way to the training ground in the afternoon, to get treatment for an injury, for example, there was his car. He lives for his work," reveals one of the players who worked with him at Coimbra.

The new-found motivation that was making itself felt among the players, had not yet spread to the club's supporters, who were not aware of the work being done, and therefore felt distant from the team. So much so that Villas-Boas's official debut as manager had no more than 866 spectators – yes, that's right, eight hundred and sixty-six – in the stands at the Cidade de Coimbra Stadium. Académica were playing Portimonense, from the Second Portuguese Division, and won 2-1 taking a step forward towards the following round of the Portuguese Cup. It was the team's very first victory in an official match in the 2009-10 season. More importantly, it was André Villas-Boas's first victory as a football manager. It was, shall we say, an auspicious beginning.

José Eduardo Simões says that although there were few supporters at the stadium, those that were there "greeted André enthusiastically. They were extremely welcoming and supportive. He came on to a great round of applause. Expectations were high, in a good sense."

But, as fate would have it, André Villas-Boas's next match, his first in the League, was to be against the club so dear to his heart, and at the Dragon Stadium no less. Only ten short days after having started work at Coimbra, he already had very well defined ideas about how the team should organise itself on the pitch. Was that to mean that playing against the "great" FC Porto, full of stars, lowly Académica would opt for the man-to-man marking so typical of Portuguese football?

The young manager's press conference statement was assertive. "No way. For me, man-to-man marking doesn't exist. I don't believe in that type of marking. I prefer pressure areas and space limitation." And he continued simply: "If my team presses the way I'd like it to and limits the action areas of the opposition's players, then we're already halfway along the road to a good result."

It was a close win for FC Porto (3-2), particularly as the last of the Dragons' goals came from an offside. Despite the defeat, the way that the team responded spurred the manager on. Faithful to his maxim that with him all players started from scratch, in that very match he gave opportunities to several who had rarely been used by the previous coach.

Portuguese football began to get to know a new sports personality and so began the numerous (and inevitable) comparisons with José Mourinho. At this stage they were still mostly restricted to Villas-Boas's appearances at press conferences: the same way of dressing, the same 3-day stubble, the same sort of approach and language, the same attitude, the same confidence. An interesting, intelligent and good-humoured presentation, but very pragmatic at the same time.

And an improvement could already be seen in the team. Académica welcomed the "European" Vitória de Guimarães in Coimbra for the next league match. They were in desperate need of a win, and win they did, by a solid 2-0. Académica were impressive, especially because of the calmness and confidence that they showed – something that was particularly surprising from a team that was bottom of the League.

SPORTING... ALREADY?... !?

At around this time (November 2009), some 200 kilometres away from Coimbra, yet another crisis struck one of Portugal's three "major" teams: Sporting's manager Paulo Bento (currently Portugal's national coach), the director of football, Pedro Barbosa (a charismatic former Sporting player), and the principal administrator of their SAD (Society of Soccer Sports), Miguel Ribeiro Teles, all resigned at the very same time. Just a little over three weeks after signing with Académica and with only three matches under his belt, André Villas-Boas was the person chosen by the Lions' president, José Eduardo Bettencourt, to succeed Paulo

Bento. Other names were mentioned in the press – such as José Pekerman, Co Adriense and Juande Ramos – but Sporting's real target was to reach agreement with André Villas-Boas.

It is said that this was not the first time that Sporting had thought of the young coach. The club's former president, Filipe Soares Franco, had weighed up the possibilities of taking a gamble on André Villas-Boas if he ran and won the June 2009 elections and if Paulo Bento were not up to continuing as manager at the end of the season. In the end, Soares Franco didn't run for club president, José Eduardo Bettencourt won a landslide victory and Paulo Bento stayed on at Sporting.

In November 2009, the person who most decisively influenced president Bettencourt to take a gamble on André Villas-Boas was Ricardo Sá Pinto [17]. The two had known each other, albeit not very well, for a few years, but had become good friends when Sá Pinto spent a week in Milan on an internship with José Mourinho, as he sought to learn from the work that was being carried out at Inter. They became such good friends that André Villas-Boas invited the former Sporting player to join his coaching staff when he very nearly signed as manager of Sporting de Braga.

As soon as Sporting's interest in him became public knowledge, Villas-Boas made a point of saying that he wanted the matter to be dealt with in "the English way". His contract with Académica had a release clause which required a payment of 500,000 Euros. However, the clause could only be activated at the end of each season, and so it would take more than Sporting depositing 500,000 Euros in Académica's bank account to release him from his contract. Consequently, Villas-Boas wanted Sporting to first contact

---

17. *Ricardo Sá Pinto was one of Sporting's most charismatic players. Though temperamental, he established a relationship of great empathy with the fans, especially with the Juventude Leonina, Sporting's principal supporters' club. He was director of professional football at Sporting between November 2009 and January 2010. He returned at the beginning of the 2011-12 season to coach the club's youth team.*

the club with whom he was contracted and try to come to an agreement with them.

It was not difficult to reach agreement between Sporting and André Villas-Boas. The meeting between the club and André's FIFA agent, Carlos Gonçalves[18], set out practically everything, including the young manager's salary, which would rise from the circa 100 thousand Euros he had received at Académica to around 300 thousand Euros with Sporting. There were only a few other details left to iron out.

According to the press, the decision was in the hands of the president of Académica. For his part, Villas-Boas said he was flattered by the interest and had already started looking for assistants to accompany him for the move from Coimbra to Lisbon.

The very same press said that in exchange, José Eduardo Simões wanted one million Euros and three players from Sporting's squad, two on loan and one permanently (Saleiro). According to what was said at the time, Sporting wouldn't agree and neither side would back down. The agreement with Villas-Boas went up in smoke, and they chose instead to sign Carlos Carvalhal, a coach who was unemployed at the time and was more usually to be seen commentating on television.

But José Eduardo Simões disagrees with this version of the story and says that "Académica and Sporting did, in fact, come to an agreement. But Sporting and André Villas-Boas were not in total agreement regarding objectives and positions."

André Villas-Boas, who already had his coaching staff practically all lined up, went back on his decision to move to Alvalade and apparently left Sá Pinto "hanging", as the latter tried

---

18. *Carlos Gonçalves is an economist born in Lisbon in January 1970. Owner of the company Proeleven, where his brother Vítor also works, he has been a FIFA agent since 2001. His relationship with André Villas-Boas began in Lisbon, when both attended a sports management course sponsored by the Dutchman Johan Cruyff. He has a portfolio of 60 players, but none that can be considered a top player at international level.*

to reach him on the telephone, but in vain. It was Carlos Gonçalves who told Sporting's new director of football that Villas-Boas had decided to stay on at Coimbra, even though he felt "very honoured" by Sporting's interest.

Sources close to Sá Pinto say that Villas-Boas's move to Sporting did not take place because Bettencourt thought that the investment in the young manager was too high, but also because André had decided to remain at Coimbra, "perhaps for emotional reasons" or because he thought that "it was still too soon to take such a great leap in his career."

In the meantime, as a result of the work carried out by Villas-Boas, Académica had now moved from bottom place in the League and were steadily making their way up the table. In January, by the end of the first half of the season, they had moved into a more comfortable tenth position (15 matches, 4 wins, 4 draws and 7 defeats, 20 goals for and 27 against).

They had an individual way of playing, and a well-defined style, which Luís Freitas Lobo defined as follows in his weekly column in the prestigious sports daily *A Bola*: "The basis is in the organisation, the factor that has changed the positional play of the squad. Players closer together, more short passes, more possession. There is less of the speed of stretching play through counter-attack because he doesn't try, as a matter of principle, to create the spaces in which to release the long ball. He has understood that this would mean losing the ball more quickly."

THE HUMAN FACTOR

Manuel Sérgio, the professor referred to earlier as quoting the training of a pianist in relation to "tactical periodisation", was the first to predict the success that José Mourinho would achieve as a football coach. He was his professor at the Higher Institute of

Physical Education, and he left such a mark on the future coach that Mourinho immediately chose him to write the preface for the only official book on him, entitled "José Mourinho" [19]. In that preface, and at a time when Mourinho had not yet won anything as a manager (although he was close to doing so at FC Porto), Manuel Sérgio wrote: "As a football coach, José Mourinho is, for me, on the same level as a Maradona or a Pelé! Am I exaggerating? Only time (the great master!) will prove me right. But I will wait, patiently!"

He was not wrong nor did he have to wait very long. Time has indeed proven him right.

In Lisbon, Manuel Sérgio was also following, from a distance, the work being carried out by Villas-Boas. He decided to write to him, remarking that, given a club with the necessary and suitable conditions, the young André would go on to become an exceptional coach. Villas-Boas was hugely surprised by the letter, especially given who it was from – someone who had once been internationally introduced as one of Mourinho's "gurus". He promptly phoned the professor.

– I'd like to know why you see me as having a brilliant future as a football coach. I feel I have so much to learn!

– Because you, my friend, know how to lead a team, you know how to communicate with the players, you know to read a match, you live tensely and intensely seek victory. This is the basis of what brings success as a high competition coach. This is what I see, even on the television. With the structural support of a great club and with what you have learnt from José Mourinho, my friend you will have tenfold the amount of the talent you're showing.

As with José Mourinho, the "old" professor wasn't wrong in his assessment of the future success of André Villas-Boas.

---

19. *"José Mourinho", written by Mourinho himself and Luís Lourenço, his childhood friend, was first published in 2003 by Portuguese publisher Prime Books. An updated edition was published in the UK by Dewi Lewis Media in 2004 and has been translated into various languages.*

This first contact led to a growing relationship between the two, and a desire on the part of André Villas-Boas to continue talking to Manuel Sérgio so as to better understand what the latter had been advocating since 1979: his theory of complexity applied to sport. Basically, this theory argues that everything functions as part of a network, that everything is related to everything else, and nothing can be looked at on its own. If we remember what has already been said about "tactical periodisation", it is easy to understand that, essentially, this approach to coaching is based on the concept of complexity.

Over various telephone conversations, Manuel Sérgio had the opportunity to explain to Villas-Boas that, at the root of everything, is the understanding that this area of knowledge, more than being a physical activity, is a human activity. That is, the human factor is always the most important. And therefore, a coach, any coach, during his moments of reflection, must ask himself the following question: what type of person do I want to be created from the players I lead? According to Manuel Sérgio, it is through this question that the essential moment in training can be found. "Because in football a player must develop himself in a team, without being reduced to the team."

"And so," stresses Manuel Sérgio, "the player must believe in what he does and transform himself into the expression of faith that uplifts the entire club, from the most humble of club members and workers to the members of the Board." He goes on to add that "belief generates biology. The player who believes he is one of the essential aspects of the soul of a club has greater strength and greater speed and greater stamina and greater driving force, etc."

How important were the "teachings" of Manuel Sérgio in the process of André Villas-Boas's development as a coach? As a reader, you will draw your own conclusions as you read this book and are better able to understand the way in which André works with, and relates to, his players – that is to say, the relevance that he gives to the human factor. But also the importance he places on the freedom he always wants his players to have so as to develop within the team.

He mentioned the human factor when he was commentating on Portugal's convincing 4-0 win over World Champions, Spain. It was a victory based on a side, which despite having more or less the same group of players, had changed considerably following Paulo Bento's replacement of Carlos Queiroz as national coach. "I can only compare what has happened with the Portuguese side to the experience I had at Académica. It is the same group of players, but under this new leadership they have regained their motivation. As Professor Manuel Sérgio wrote in *A Bola*, this is a human sciences activity, and perhaps this is why this same group, apart from one or two players, had recently been eliminated by Spain yet now managed to win 4-0. It's a group that has found its balance, that looks at itself differently, that transcends itself and finds in the image of its leader a person of reference, which perhaps did not happen before. Or rather, I don't know if it happened or not, what I know is that this happened to me at Académica, where it was not only *my* daily work that brought about a great change."

In relation to the role that he likes to see his players carry out, he recently told the *Sunday Mirror* that "I am not a dictator as I encourage freedom of choice among my players. They can only achieve their true potential if they are not shackled. Creativity in my players is important. I love the unpredictable part of the game. I strongly believe that players have to express themselves, they must be able to make choices during the game".

In one of his telephone conversations with Manuel Sérgio when it was already possible to foresee the success he would achieve at FC Porto, André Villas-Boas admitted to the "old" philosopher: "You believed in me even before I did!" And this was certainly true.

A VERY POSITIVE ATMOSPHERE

All those surrounding André Villas-Boas at Académica could see that the young manager was actually building a particularly close relationship with his players. He would speak to them, but not only about football-related matters. He would ask about their personal life, and he was interested in everything related to them. He encouraged lunches and dinners with the entire working group, and sometimes even footed the bill!

These get-togethers usually took place at the restaurant, *O Telheiro*. Situated less than 500 metres from the Academy where Académica trains, close to the city's old station, it is owned by the young and friendly Miguel Lopes. It serves mainly grilled food and is famed and sought-out for its Brazilian Picanha, sirloin steak grilled over open flames.

Apart from these get-togethers, Villas-Boas was a regular customer at *O Telheiro*. After the morning practices, he would often have lunch there, usually with his assistants. He almost always had grilled fish – which the restaurant orders on a daily basis from suppliers in Figueira da Foz – with a little wine, and dessert to round off the meal. He was very communicative, and was always joking with the restaurant owner because his favourite club was Benfica. In short, he was a down-to-earth and friendly guy, who captivated everyone he came into contact with there.

Whether or not as a result of frequent visits by Académica's professionals, but certainly because of its great quality of service and the well-priced grilled dishes it serves, *O Telheiro* is today one of the most popular restaurants in Coimbra and unless you have booked you will definitely be in for a very long wait. One of its walls boasts a framed and eye-catching number six Chelsea shirt, autographed by Ricardo Carvalho, but given with kindness and friendship by André Villas-Boas!

Apart from *O Telheiro*, Académica's young manager was also a regular at another restaurant, *O Moinho Velho*, situated close to the stadium and his apartment. He had lunch there on several occasions with the club president and other members of the coaching staff. The simple way in which he interacted with everyone there was a characteristic greatly appreciated by all.

Back to the work he carried out, the young manager continued to assert himself and sought to relay information to the players in a very concise and structured way, avoiding the lengthy lectures and long and tiring videos that they so dislike. A former member of the club confided that, "There were usually two preparation talks for each match. On the Thursday or Friday, he would dedicate himself completely to analysing the opponent we'd be playing against. By means of a 30-minute video, he'd give us all the information about our next opponent. On matchday itself, he'd only talk about our team."

AVB would also frequently ask the players questions. He wanted to know whether they felt comfortable with the tactical system he intended to use. This is something very close to what Mourinho calls "guided discovery".

However, the creativity and unpredictability that Villas-Boas so greatly appreciates did not mean he was less careful when preparing for training or matches – on the contrary. As Markus Berger[20] confided, "each training session was very specific in terms of preparing us for the next match. We never had two training sessions a day, only one in the morning, but it was always very intense."

According to Berger, Villas-Boas was very demanding. "He demanded 100% from the players, and then some. He wanted our maximum concentration and he prepared each practice with a great deal of quality. We knew every detail about our opponents. He did everything to make it easy for the players; he identified the strengths and weaknesses of our opponents' defence, midfield and

---

20. *Markus Berger, 26 year-old Austrian player, central defender at Académica, in an interview to the BBC.*

attack, as well as which of the opposing players could make the difference. And he read the game very well."

Something which Villas-Boas already used to emphasise at that stage was the importance of passing. The Austrian player has an interesting detail to share with us: "He would often have us training in very tight spaces, where you cannot have the ball in your possession for very long. As a central defender, he would encourage me to move the ball around and he would talk to each player about the type of passes he wanted them to make."

The players at Académica appreciated Villas-Boas's methods, particularly the discrete way he would bring to their attention any mistake they had made, never reprimanding them in public, nor looking for culprits when faced with a defeat. He would take them aside and calmly tell them what he was after so that they clearly understood him. Although extremely kind and understanding, he nevertheless demanded their all. And he was never satisfied, always wanting more and more. He boosted their self-esteem and raised their confidence levels by means of his powerful ability to motivate. As the president of the club confirmed: "He created a very positive working atmosphere around him." So much so, that even the players who weren't a part of his team selection were satisfied – something extremely rare in the football world.

He only had one truly serious case of indiscipline, when the player Diogo Gomes was caught enjoying a night out; and he resolved it within the working group. André Villas-Boas did not punish the player, but he confronted him about it in front of the team and the technical staff. He did not want a repeat situation. In an interview to the *Diário de Coimbra* he later explained: "Within our leadership, also partly because we're a young technical team, open leadership is fundamental. That involves players taking direct responsibility, a great deal of straightforwardness and the players being able to have a valid opinion on the management of the group. In this particular instance, the group gave its opinion and reproved Diogo's actions. The matter was resolved internally, within the group, with no disciplinary action from the Board. The group reproached the player and decided what action needed taking. This type of leadership is not always possible, but it's the type of leadership with which we identify."

Another very particular way of interacting with his players is through text messages. Villas-Boas is addicted to texting. For example, one of the players was informed first hand by the coach that he had been selected for the Portuguese national team in a text, where André also took the opportunity to congratulate him on being called up. Another player who had a problem with his knees remembers receiving a text asking him to make a sacrifice for the two matches they still had left to play.

Such was the personal relationship he had with the players, that even after he had left Académica he continued exchanging texts with them. He might not reply to texts immediately, but no text goes unanswered – even today. He has always made players feel that they can contact him about any issue.

But the young coach who, as everyone will readily attest to, is obsessed with football and thinks about it round the clock, also had the opportunity to show his human side and the qualities of a great leader when misfortune dramatically knocked at the door of one of his players. The forward Miguel Pedro lost twins when they were born prematurely, and Villas-Boas did everything he could to try to provide comfort and help. He immediately went to the hospital to keep up with the situation and to offer his support. He arranged for doctors he knew to be on hand for Pedro's wife and, after the tragedy, he was tireless in his support of the player. "He told him to go home and to come back when he was ready. While Miguel Pedro was away, he always kept in touch with him. He even spoke to people he knew at a clinic, to provide the help that Miguel's wife needed so that she could become pregnant again as quickly as possible," explained a former colleague.

This was not an isolated case. When a relative of a player from Madeira passed away, Villas-Boas told him to fly out to the island and to return only when he felt ready to do so. "He believes that when a player isn't there mentally, then it is best to go to where his worries are, and to come back only when he feels able to concentrate on work, when he has cleared his head," the same player explained.

He took a strong stand when it came to defending his staff, the team and the club. His disagreement with José Gomes, Jesualdo Ferreira's assistant coach at FC Porto, made headlines as the two had a heated exchange during the half-time interval of the match between the two clubs. It was only the rapid intervention of several members of both technical teams that stopped it from becoming a more serious incident.

SPORTING ONCE AGAIN

At the beginning of February 2010, Villas-Boas's Académica finally savoured its first victory in an away match in the League. And it wasn't at any old stadium. It wasn't at the stadium of a modest team, one of those teams that were Académica's direct competitors in the struggle to avoid relegation. A surprising win? Yes, but totally deserved. A win against one of the three "big" teams in Portuguese football, to be more precise at Alvalade – the home of Sporting!

"At half-time the score was 1-1, excellent for us. But, contrary to what you'd expect, Villas-Boas was furious when he got to the changing room. He made it very clear that he would rather lose by four, but have the team play as he wanted them to. And basically he wanted more ball possession. The result was that we played an extraordinary second half and beat Sporting by 2-1!" confided one of the first choice players from that Saturday night. Sporting were already in the middle of a crisis because of their disappointing results. Now Villas-Boas helped to turn what was already a bad situation into an unbearable one.

As a result, José Eduardo Bettencourt decided that Carlos Carvalhal's contract would not be renewed at the end of the season. In fact, in one of his well-known "shots in the foot", the Lions' president had publicly stated that the continuation of Carlos Carvalhal (who had been signed provisionally) at the club, depended solely on the team's results. And once again he turned to André Villas-Boas as he sought to secure him for the 2010-11 season, resulting in a written agreement between the parties.

Carvalhal found out from a trustworthy source that Sporting had contacted Villas-Boas. Unsurprisingly he wasn't happy, particularly as the process was taking place at a crucial time in the season, with absolutely decisive matches still left to play. He even cancelled a press conference as he felt he could not face a group of journalists with a barrage of questions about the future – his and the club's.

And, at the beginning of March 2010, a joint statement was issued by the manager and the board at Académica with the objective, according to José Eduardo Simões, "of bringing under control all the false information that was circulating". The statement denied that there was any agreement with Sporting. However, given the work he was carrying out and the visibility earned by the team's results, it was clear that Villas-Boas would not be staying on as Académica's manager after the end of June 2010.

On the penultimate day of March, Sporting finally announced that they would not renew Carlos Carvalhal's contract at the end of the season, and sent a statement to the CMVM[21], making the future departure of the manager official.

Consequently the media's intense pressure on Académica's

---

21. *CMVM are the initials of the Comissão do Mercado de Valores Mobiliários – the Portuguese Securities Market Commission. Clubs listed on the Stock Exchange, such as Sporting, Benfica and FC Porto, are obliged to notify the CMVM of all decisions that may influence the prices of their shares.*

young manager resumed, to the extent that in the press conference before the match with União de Leira, he stated ironically: "I'm enjoying the fact that there are so many journalists present – just for a match against Leiria, I know only too well who comes here week after week." And to finish off: "The others are here to keep the circus going!"

The agreement between the manager and Sporting had been drawn up with the mediation of the powerful FIFA agent and Gestifute[22] boss, Jorge Mendes, who had already helped the club following the reopening of the transfer market. From that moment on, the only concern would be to keep everything under wraps while preparations for the 2010-11 season got underway.

However, Villas-Boas, with the consent of José Eduardo Bettencourt, put an end to everything within a matter of days. Apparently it was because he had had several differences of opinion with the former FC Porto midfielder, Costinha, who had just been appointed Director of Football at Sporting, but also because it was around then that FC Porto had started showing an interest in him.

In his defence, José Eduardo Simões says that Villas-Boas "has a very clear idea of how communication should work. The entire chain, from the president to the employees, has to work with a single voice. It is only in Portugal that everyone talks about football. He is very professional, very demanding, he wants to see everybody imbued with the same spirit and, in this context, communication is a most important aspect. Clubs that work this way, win, the others don't." So, if we think about how Sporting worked and how FC Porto has always worked, and add to that the passion the manager had always felt for Porto, it is easy to understand why he chose to turn his back on Sporting so as to begin negotiations with Pinto da Costa's club.

---

22. Founded by Jorge Mendes, Gestifute provides agent services for footballers. Portugal allows third parties to own part of the economic rights of the players, and to receive a share of transfer fees.

And so, Sporting once again contacted the CMVM, this time on 5 April, to notify them that André Villas-Boas would not be the club's manager for the 2010-11 season. They implied that it was the club that had broken off the agreement – and not Villas-Boas. They had not liked the term "circus" which the manager had used when referring to the possibility of coaching Sporting.

Académica finished the season in 11th place, with eight wins, nine draws and thirteen defeats, 37-42 in goals. That is, in 23 matches in charge of the team, Villas-Boas had eight wins, six draws and nine defeats. Not so bad for a team that had been bottom of the League, and whom everybody thought were definitely headed for relegation.

The president of Académica says he is convinced that if Villas-Boas had joined them at the very beginning of the season, the club would probably have finished in the top five. And he is unsparing in his compliments for the coach to whom he first gave the opportunity of becoming a manager: "I could tell after our first meeting that he is a great human being and a natural leader."

As for André's meteoric passage at Académica, José Eduardo Simões recalls: "He has got talent and he is very easy to work with. He creates a good atmosphere. He communicates well, has a clear and well-structured message, he likes 'mind-games' and makes good use of them. He knows what he wants and how to achieve it." He went on to add that "he is not about screaming or whipping. He is a very good psychologist, he knows how to gain someone's trust, and he gets into each individual and draws him into the group."

As he was living alone in Coimbra, he had "great availability" and "was most endearing even to people outside the club," concludes José Eduardo Simões. "Since he moved to London, I have become a 'specialist' in André Villas-Boas!" the Académica president added, joking about the media blitz he has experienced since it was announced that Villas-Boas would replace the Italian, Carlo Ancelotti, at Chelsea.

The young coach recently said that he viewed the leap he has taken – from scout to manager – as natural. "The opportunity to coach came up when I was at Inter. I felt I wanted to carry out other functions; I rose to the challenge and went to Académica, leaving José (Mourinho). Coaching was not an obsession, and I did not use Mourinho to follow this path. It's something that happened naturally," he declared.

Académica definitely left its mark on André Villas-Boas. After he had been appointed manager of FC Porto he acknowledged the debt and gratitude that he felt to the club.

"Being the sentimental person that I am, going back to Coimbra stirs a host of emotions in me. Since the start of the season (2010-11), I've been there three times. It wasn't possible to meet up with everyone, but I was with people who mean a great deal to me, and to whom I am truly thankful."

4

IN THE "DREAM SEAT"

*"I knew we would celebrate (the league title) because
I knew him, because I saw that he had been born for football
and I knew his ability. I knew he had what it takes to
be a successful manager, and in addition to all of that
he is as much a Dragon as all of us."*

Jorge Nuno Pinto da Costa

In Coimbra, Villas-Boas was scoring points during his first experience as manager at the modest Académica, working to keep the
team from relegation, an objective he achieved. In Porto, Jesualdo
Ferreira – coach at FC Porto since 2006-07 – was becoming increas-
ingly aware that his team would not retain the title of Portuguese
champions in the 2009-10 season. This was a particularly
significant title as it would have meant FC Porto becoming five
times champions for the second time in the club's history and in the
history of Portuguese football. Jesualdo Ferreira's time at FC Porto
was therefore coming to an end, even though there was still another
year left on his contract, and despite the fact that they were likely to
win another trophy, the Portuguese Cup, given that their opponents
in the final were Grupo Desportivo de Chaves, a weak team from
the Second League.

In the previous three seasons, as FC Porto's manager, Ferreira
had won three League titles, two Cups (in the end, he won three) and
a Super Cup. This would almost certainly have been more than
enough to assure his continuation as manager at any other club in
the world. Not so at FC Porto, where winning the League is normal
and losing it is abnormal. In fact, over the last ten years, from
2001-02 to 2010-11, FC Porto have won seven championships; in

the last 20 years they have won 14; and since Pinto da Costa became president 28 years ago, they have won the Champions' League twice, the UEFA cup twice, a European Super Cup, two intercontinental cups, as well as 18 Portuguese League titles, 12 Portuguese Cups and 16 Portuguese Super Cups. An enviable CV, which has led most observers to attribute FC Porto's victories more to the sports management skills of its historic president and the solid winning culture he has implemented, than to the coaches that he has training the team.

Jesualdo, who was on his way to a fifth season as FC Porto's manager, was used to the way things worked at the club, and he began to notice certain behaviour that led him to believe he would probably not be staying on. The first indicator of an imminent divorce came in February 2010. Usually, at around that time of the year, meetings would be taking place to prepare the squad for the following season, to look for reinforcements and to outline the pre-season plan. But neither Pinto da Costa, nor Antero Henrique[23] spoke to Jesualdo about these matters. This was the first sign. As time went by, nobody discussed anything with him.

At the same time, in the corridors of football – which are deep, very deep – the name of André Villas-Boas began to be heard. The information that reached Pinto da Costa on the work he was carrying out at Académica seemed to make up for the fact that he did not as yet have much managerial experience.

Not once did anybody hear Pinto da Costa publicly mention André Villas-Boas. Usually, when the president of FC Porto compliments a coach, it is because he has his eye on him. This happened with Fernando Santos, Jesualdo Ferreira, and even with Carlos Queiroz, who only didn't end up at the Dragon Stadium because he'd already made a committment to the Portuguese Football Federation to become coach of the national team. But the

---

23. *Antero Henrique is Pinto da Costa's right-hand man, and the General Director of FC Porto's SAD (Society of Soccer Sports).*

name André was never mentioned at the Dragon... not even to be denied. Looking back, it is clear that many dismissed the name of Mourinho's former scout because Pinto da Costa wasn't paying him compliments.

In May 2010, just before another significant achievement by Jesualdo Ferreira, who secured his third consecutive Portuguese Cup, Pinto da Costa won the elections for club president. It was uncontested and he received 98% of the votes. His new plans for FC Porto involved the implementation of various changes, in relation to both the SAD (Society of Soccer Sports) and to the technical team. The restructuring even went so far as to affect a historic figure at Porto – Reinaldo Teles, a member of the Board, and a faithful lifelong friend of Pinto da Costa. Although he was to remain at the club, he would no longer be close to the football team. In addition, the re-elected president already had a profile for the next manager: young, a believer in a more scientific philosophy, and blue-blooded. Jesualdo Ferreira, at 60 plus, was definitely on his way out. André Villas-Boas, an ardent fan of the club since childhood, fitted the profile set out by the Porto president like a glove.

Despite the numerous names speculated on in the media, that of André Villas-Boas had always been on Pinto da Costa's mind from the moment he had decided not to continue with Jesualdo Ferreira. Another of the president's customs is to let names pop up in the press, sometimes even leaked out by him. And so many coaches, both Portuguese and foreign, were linked to FC Porto. Two particularly worthy of note were Domingos Paciência and Jorge Costa, both symbols of the club, with short – albeit very successful – careers as managers. It has also been said that Jorge Costa was even contacted later about him being Villas-Boas's number two.

There are those that say Villas-Boas turned down Sporting in April 2010 mainly because of interest from FC Porto. There are those who say that knowing how FC Porto works, and the way that Sporting worked at that time, the choice of the young manager was understandable. But if you then add his indisputable love of all things Porto – "Porto is my city, FC Porto was, is and always will be my club," he would later state when he was presented at Chelsea – then, in his place, only a madman would have chosen to manage Sporting.

So, by mid May 2010, André Villas-Boas had come to a verbal agreement with FC Porto. Only one thing worried him: that the news might get out and that this might put pressure on the club to renege on the agreement. Consequently, he denied all speculation and even stopped taking phone calls, other than from the friends he usually spoke to. He was so careful that not even his family knew anything about it.

However, the decision to choose the young manager from Académica was not welcomed by everyone at Porto. People close to the president wanted to have Villas-Boas, but those even closer to Pinto da Costa were not at all keen on that possibility. There were those who saw in him the successor to Mourinho, but there were also those who were extremely wary as he was too young and hadn't yet proved himself sufficiently to take on the position of manager at a club of the size and with the responsibilities of FC Porto.

Furthermore, at the top of the club's hierarchy, there were those who made a point of recalling the rather undiplomatic manner in which André, along with José Mourinho, had left the club for Chelsea at the end of the 2003-04 season. Worse still was the knowledge that he had come to the Dragon accompanied by several private security guards when he returned to observe FC Porto, Chelsea's future opponents in the Champions League. The club also hadn't liked the fact that on the day he left with Mourinho, and under the latter's orders, André had emptied his locker and taken the many reports that, although written by him, were nonetheless the property of FC Porto. Thus, the name of Villas-Boas was far from consensual, but as always happens at the club, if Pinto da Costa was to eventually decide on Villas-Boas, then nobody doubted that he would be presented to the press and the fans and immediately accepted by all the critics.

Truth be told, it is always Pinto da Costa who takes the final decision, and he needs no support to do so. It is he who chooses the managers, and it is he who takes full responsibility should things go wrong. He hasn't had to very often, as he usually makes very good choices. In fact, throughout his long reign, he has already taken a gamble on ten managers who did not have a single title to their name when they arrived at FC Porto. Among these, seven emerged victorious: Artur Jorge, António Oliveira, Fernando Santos, José Mourinho, Co Adriense, Jesualdo Ferreira and André Villas-Boas. And three won international titles: Artur Jorge (the European Champions Cup in 1987), José Mourinho (the UEFA Cup in 2003 and the Champions League in 2004) and André Villas-Boas (the Europa League in 2011).

Anyone who knows Pinto da Costa also knows that before announcing a new head of the coaching staff, he would personally, and with great dignity, take care of terminating the contract of Jesualdo Ferreira. And this is indeed what happened. On his return to Porto after a short holiday, he quickly arranged for the contractual relationship between the manager and the club to be terminated in a befittingly friendly way. There followed a period of 'mourning', a few days' strategic silence before the presentation of André Villas-Boas as the youngest-ever manager at FC Porto, at just 32 years of age. Académica, with whom Villas-Boas was on contract for one more season, received the 500,000 Euros stipulated by the release clause in the contract between the club and the manager.

Villas-Boas was aware that he was taking on a very heavy burden. Firstly, because of the club's incredibly successful past – and that of his predecessors – with its consequent obligation to achieve immediate results. Secondly, because arch-rivals Benfica seemed to be set on a new cycle of domination in Portuguese football following their convincing victory in the 2009-10 Championship. It was therefore absolutely imperative for FC Porto to recover the League Title that they had lost in the current season. And finally, because FC Porto, keeping to what seems to have become an annual tradition of alienating two or three of its most important players[24], were getting ready to pocket 20 million Euros from the sale of Bruno Alves to Zenith St. Petersburg and a further 13 million as Raul Meireles headed for Liverpool FC. Bruno Alves was team captain at the time – and, of course, captains are crucially important in keeping a balance in the dressing room of any club – and Raul Meireles was one of the vice captains. Added to that Nuno Espírito Santo, the third goalkeeper, and another changing room leader, was hanging up his boots and bringing his career as a professional footballer to an end. He was on his way to Malaga, to join Jesualdo Ferreira's future technical team.

However, in his favour, André had a great advantage over Ferreira, who had spent two years having to speak both on his behalf and on behalf of the club, defending issues related to the corruption scandal – Apito Dourado (Golden Whistle)[25] – which had rocked Portuguese football. As he himself was under investigation, the club

24. In the last few years only, FC Porto has sold (amounts in Euros): 2004 Ricardo Carvalho (Chelsea, 30 million), Paulo Ferreira (Chelsea, 20 million), Deco (Barcelona, 15 million plus Ricardo Quaresma), Derlei (Dynamo Moscow, 8 million) and... José Mourinho (Chelsea, 6 million); 2005 Maniche (Dynamo Moscow, 16 million), Costinha (Dynamo Moscow,4 million), Seitaridis (Dynamo Moscow, 10 million) and Luis Fabiano (Seville, 2.5 million); 2006 Diego (Werder Bremen, 6 million) and McCarthy (Blackburn Rovers, 4 million) ; 2007 Pepe (Real Madrid, 30 million), Anderson (Man. United, 30 million), Hugo Almeida (Werder Bremen, 6 million) and Ricardo Costa (Wolfsburg, 5 million); 2008 Ricardo Quaresma (Inter, 18.6 million plus Pelé) and Bosingwa (Chelsea, 20.5 million); 2009 Lucho Gonzalez (Marseille, 18 million), Lisandro Lopez (Lyon, 24 million), Cissoko (Lyon, 15 million) and Ibson (Spartak Moscow, 5 million); 2010 Bruno Alves (Zenith, 22 million) and Raul Meireles (Liverpool, 13 million).
25. Apito Dourado (The Golden Whistle) was a sports corruption scandal that rocked Portuguese football in 2004. The most well-known people under investigation were Pinto da Costa (president of FC Porto) and Major Valentim Loureiro (former president of Boavista and, up until the present date, president of the Club League). They were subsequently acquitted by the civil courts.

president, Pinto da Costa, wasn't able to say anything about it and therefore the former manager had had to fight off many attacks. The arrival of André Villas-Boas coincided with Pinto da Costa being released from these legal restrictions, and being once again able to respond to issues related to the suspicions raised about FC Porto. Nevertheless, at his press conferences, André Villas-Boas always came across as an important acolyte, showing his support for the president and, at times, taking a stance as if he were a fan. But the simple fact that the president could once again speak freely was a huge point in Villas-Boas's favour. In Portugal, Pinto da Costa's public words carry great weight and impact significantly on the course of events at the club, and often even on Portuguese football.

But, after an apparent "to and fro", which even included what might be called a "politically correct" statement from Villas-Boas denying he was moving to the club, on 2 June 2010, FC Porto officially confirmed his signing for two seasons, and duly notified the CMVM (Portuguese Securities Market Commission). It was a high-risk decision that represented a total break with the recent past. Villas-Boas had not yet proved anything, and therein lay the risk. But, truth be told, José Mourinho himself also hadn't proved anything when he had arrived at the club. Mourinho, who knew Villas-Boas better than anybody else, dismissed this and other similarilties that were raised about him and his former scout. He even went on to question the validity of the field work that had led to Villas-Boas being chosen by FC Porto.

MOURINHO? NO, ROBSON!

The following day, the public presentation was held in the VIP room at the Dragon Stadium. André Villas-Boas and Pinto da Costa were alone, before a battalion of reporters. The young manager knew that the obvious question, about comparisons with Mourinho, would come up at any moment. It was just a matter of time. So, his answer was clear and on the tip of his tongue: "I am not a clone of anybody, but if you want to talk about this, I think I am more a clone of Robson than of Mourinho. I have English ancestry, a big nose and I like drinking wine…" In this way he immediately started distancing himself from JoséMourinho – with whom he hadn't been on very good terms since he arrived at FC Porto – and took the opportunity to make a heartfelt reference to Sir Bobby Robson, the very first coach to give him an opportunity in the football world.

In fact, Robson left an indelible mark on the young André. The Chelsea manager makes a point of emphasising this at every opportunity he gets. "Bobby was a very important person in my career and a great inspiration. No other coach would ever have done what he did, they would never have allowed a 17 year-old kid to confront them with the decisions they'd taken as coaches. He was an amazingly open person. He was the person who advised me at a very young age to go on coaching courses. He unlocked the doors of Porto for me to have access to his training sessions. We had a very good relationship, and I respected him a lot. What he did, not only with me and José (Mourinho), but with all different kinds of people, promoting them and inspiring them to follow their own way." He has stated this on various occasions. It was a relationship which left its mark and it befits the young manager to acknowledge it and be thankful for it. It is, nevertheless, strange that little attention was given to Mourinho when he spoke of the importance that people he had worked with had had on his training and development, and on his (up until now) meteoric and extremely successful career as a football manager.

As for the risks he was running by accepting the challenge of heading a team with the ambitions of FC Porto, André Villas-Boas answered assertively: "Where others may see risks, I always see a good chance of being successful. For the longest time, FC Porto has had this winning culture and I feel at home with the demands." And for those who insisted on seeing him as the new Mourinho, he explained that "promising reminds me a great deal of 2002, when a certain someone made a promise for the first time. Now, promises are made at the first conference and many promises are never kept." This is an obvious reference to the press conference at FC Porto in 2002 when José Mourinho was presented as manager, and where he stated that he was certain the club would be champions the following season – and to the positive impact those words had, so much so that many coaches, when being presented, choose to make identical promises, that are often impossible to keep.

He also had time to address those who doubted him: "Are many people sceptical of me? I admit they are, since names only become a matter of agreement when they start winning. But four or five weeks from now, I'll already be more popular." Finally, as to the team's future style of play, he explained: "Everything is completely defined, both for the training sessions and for the matches. Incompetent I am not. Everything has been thought out so as to make the team work in a certain style and always in a balanced manner."

The night before he had publicly bid farewell to the president, directors, employees, players and members of Académica. Known to be somewhat addicted to text messages, Villas-Boas made a point of sending the players a text moments before his signing with the Dragons was made public officially. It was a gesture that they all appreciated since they now knew first hand, and from the coach himself, that he would be leaving Académica. The text also conveyed a heartfelt farewell: "I'm leaving you for a new adventure. I thank you for the time we spent together. Each one of you has made your mark at the start of my career and all in different and special ways. I wish you continued success individually and collectively, and I want you to know that I will always be available to all of you. A big hug and see you soon." Those who know the way Mourinho communicates with his players via text messages, would be hard-pressed to find a greater similarity.

While it is true that many doubted Villas-Boas had the capacity to hold the position of manager at FC Porto, there were others who knew his work well and immediately vouched for him. This was the case with Ricardo Carvalho, the central defender who had played for FC Porto and for Chelsea, and who was getting ready to make his way to Real Madrid, to once again work with Mourinho, after the World Cup in South Africa. Carvalho knew Villas-Boas very well from the time when he was a part of Mourinho's technical team, and he was unstinting in his praise: "He lives and breathes football. Football is everything to him. Sometimes, he even lives football too much. He's incredibly thorough in the reports he draws up. He can scrutinise an opponent right down to the smallest detail. Nothing gets past him. He knows everything about players, everything about teams. Someone who makes the choices he has made is someone who is not afraid to take risks. After all, he had a nice life, quietly getting on doing what he did with Mourinho, but he preferred to swap that security for something riskier. He preferred to go it alone, and if he did so it's because he is extremely confident. He is a sensible and sincere person. Trust me: he knows what he's doing. I'll be rooting for his success. He deserves it." Ricardo Carvalho, as we know today, was not wrong.

As FC Porto announced their signing of André Villas-Boas, Belenenses, a historic club from Lisbon that had just been relegated, presented Baltemar Brito as their manager. This coincidence led Ricardo Araújo Pereira, the most popular comedian in Portugal today and well-known for being a fervent Benfica fan, to come up with the following satirical text, published in the sports daily *A Bola*: "Following André Villas-Boas (seven seasons with Mourinho), Baltemar Brito (six seasons with Mourinho) is the second assistant of the Special One to be signed as manager of a Portuguese club. Belenenses, without the financial clout to pay for seven seasons of Mourinho, had to settle for six. (…) It has been said that Trofense now have their eye on José Mourinho's barber. Now, as a citizen who has already exchanged four text messages with the Special One, I would like to take this opportunity to let the market know that I am not available to coach any teams."

GETTING DOWN TO WORK

Villas-Boas's first day as manager at FC Porto, 6 June, was spent observing the club's youth teams, morning and afternoon. He immediately started to score points with the fans who, in Portugal at least, appreciate it when coaches take the time to observe the youth teams, as if acknowledging that they are there on the look-out for future football stars.

Then he set off for a week's holiday, returning to Porto on 13 June and immediately beginning work with Antero Henrique, football strong man at the Dragons, for the preparation of the 2010-11 season. He did so quietly in offices, with no public appearances, no pronouncements, and no in-depth interviews. In fact, Villas-Boas passed through his whole time at FC Porto without granting a single lengthy interview. Words from the coach were only heard at the compulsory pre- and post-match press conferences. In this regard, André mirrored Pep Guardiola, who has also not been "friendly" to reporters at Barcelona. These and other ideas about Guardiola's behaviour – Villas-Boas's greatest idol amongst currently active coaches – were gleaned from reading various books on the Catalan coach.

But let's get back to FC Porto. Anybody who thought that André Villas-Boas would carry out a revolution in the squad and that, as he was used to scouting many players, he would suggest a handful of new stars for the club, were resoundingly mistaken. Studious as he is, it can be said that he was very precise in the choice of players. He knew how to get the most out of the squad Jesualdo Ferreira had left him, without demanding major signings. Working together with Antero Henrique, who was responsible for successful signings such as Hulk, Falcao, Guarín, Álvaro Pereira, Fernando, to mention just a few, worked well and there was almost no need to reinforce the squad.

FC Porto invested almost exclusively in the renewal of contracts and this had an incredibly positive effect on the staff and team. They would however, have to face the departures of Raul Meireles and Bruno Alves, though in the previous season their performances had already dropped off, something which seemed to be aggravated by their expecting transfers at the end of the season (Alves left for the Russian team Zenith, and Meireles for Liverpool).

It didn't prove difficult to solve these two problems: from Argentina the World Cup player Otamendi arrived; and from Sporting, João Moutinho! The signing of Moutinho was a huge blow to the Lions, but a great boost for FC Porto, given that within a few short days the former Sporting captain had already shown an exceptional ability to adapt: to such an extent that Villas-Boas commented that Moutinho was, effectively, a player "à la Porto", just as Pinto da Costa had described him two days before poaching him from Alvalade.

It might not seem it, but this signing not only immediately resolved the situation of Meireles's departure, but psychologically it also knocked back Sporting, one of Porto's traditional rivals for the title.

PEDROTO AND... MOURINHO!

Twenty days later, André Villas-Boas appeared in public, next to Pinto da Costa, to observe a youth team match between FC Porto and Sporting. By appearing with Villas-Boas, the president of Porto sought to reaffirm his belief in his high-stakes gamble, while at the same time lending the new manager support. Indeed, few clubs in the world can pride themselves on offering their coaches as much protection as FC Porto does via its president. One example would be Pinto da Costa's visit to the home of coach Fernando Santos, the current Greek national coach, when despite being faced with the anger of the fans after a complicated defeat, the president nevertheless proposed extending his contract.

At the same time, and to reassure the more sceptical fans, various analogies were made to José Mourinho, as well as comparisons to José Maria Pedroto[26], given that, as coincidence would have it, the old and unforgettable "master" had started working as a coach at FC Porto when he was the very same age as André Villas-Boas.

Pedroto, who had already passed away, was not there to either agree with or refute these comparisons between him and the Dragons' new manager, but Mourinho wasted no time in contesting the legitimacy with which people compared Villas-Boas's course to his. In an interview to the sports daily *Record*, when asked to comment on FC Porto having chosen André Villas-Boas to replace Jesualdo Ferreira, he stated, "I usually say that nothing surprises me in football. It is the results that always determine whether the decisions taken were more or less correct. Many may ask why they chose someone who had never been a coach before, except for those two or three months at Académica. Everything will depend on the matches and the results. But don't compare him to me, because when I went to FC Porto I had already worked on the pitch, which is quite different. And even then, people were still very sceptical."

Mourinho's words, which were viewed as a subtle, yet vicious

---

26. *José Maria Pedroto (1928-1985) was one of the most charismatic players and, above all, coaches in the history of FC Porto. A club champion, twice as a player and twice as a coach, he returned to the Dragons when Pinto da Costa was appointed director of football (in 1976), and then later president (in 1982). Considered the main inspiration behind the strategy that led the Porto president to achieve the greatest feats – national and international – in Portuguese sports management, he is a true FC Porto legend.*

criticism of André Villas-Boas, did not lead to a similar counter-attack from the former scout. In his response he once again tried to distance himself from the shadow of his former boss, saying "It's just as well he spoke, just as well that through José Mourinho's words people now understand what I've been saying since 14 October when I was presented as the manager at Académica. I am not a clone of Mourinho. I've been trying to explain this very same thing since the day I arrived in Portugal, but you always insist on this point. Right, now we have more arguments to uphold our idea." And he continued in the same breath, without letting anyone interrupt him, with other considerations: "We don't have the same character, we don't have the same personality and we have different ways of communicating with the players. So, I think everybody is clear on this now. Well, I don't even know how many matches he had between Benfica and União de Leiria before arriving at FC Porto. We either have the same number of matches, or he has four or five more. I don't know. I have no idea."

The sports press set about enlightening Villas-Boas, and presented the final tally of matches each had under their belts as a head coach when they had arrived at Porto: in the various competitions, José Mourinho had totalled 11 official matches at Benfica and 20 at União de Leiria, a total of 31 matches; on his part, as manager of Académica, André Villas-Boas had 30 to his name. A minimal one-match difference, totally insignificant and therefore undeserving of Mourinho's comment. The Real Madrid manager was probably referring to fieldwork (work out on the pitch) that he'd carried out with Bobby Robson (at Sporting, FC Porto and Barcelona) and Louis van Gaal (also at Barcelona). Even though Villas-Boas had worked at Académica for close on eight months, and not the two or three mentioned by Mourinho, his past did not include any proper fieldwork that was worthy of the name.

The truth is that this episode laid bare the strained relations between Mourinho and Villas-Boas. They were not exactly the best of friends. While at Académica, Villas-Boas had often contacted Mourinho, even if it was just by text message. Some say that he even did so to get advice. He also frequently contacted Rui Faria about technical issues related to the planning of training sessions. But when he joined FC Porto, things changed. So much so that some time later, in April 2011, the young coach admitted he wasn't on speaking terms with José Mourinho. "It has nothing to do with the separation, because even after I left, I still spoke to him a lot when I was at Académica. A rival? No, I can't be a rival to the person who, in my opinion, will be the best coach of all time," explained Villas-Boas.

Truth be told, whenever the occasion has presented itself, he is always highly complimentary of José Mourinho. In October 2010, even before the Special One had won the FIFA World Coach of the Year Award, Villas-Boas said, "The success he continues to accumulate is absolutely abnormal, but it is the result of the quality of his work and the impressive regularity with which he wins. This clearly shows the great coach, leader and communicator that he is. According to what he does in the future, he will possibly be the best coach of all time, all depending on how long he continues in this profession. But there's no doubt that's where he is headed."

When Mourinho won the above-mentioned award, he referred to the honour as being just and proffered words very much in the same vein to what we have just read.

WORKAHOLIC

As previously mentioned, FC Porto returned to work on 2 July 2010, without very significant signings, which meant that Villas-Boas was even more in the spotlight. Under the watchful eye of the entire SAD Board which, with Pinto da Costa at the helm, was yet another public gesture of support for Villas-Boas, the young manager held a training session in which the ball was present from beginning to end; in the afternoon the usual medical tests took place.

The players learnt that Villas-Boas's working rules established that they were to arrive at the workplace well in advance of the scheduled practice time. As for his new methods, very early on he showed that he cut to the chase, and wasn't one for beating about the bush. Players felt completely at ease to seek him out, and Villas-Boas encouraged this interaction. He wanted nobody to have any doubts about the new exercises or the new tactical model he wanted to implement, a variation of the previous 4-3-3. Unlike his predecessor, who was reserved and cultivated a sense of distance from the players, there wasn't much of a barrier between André and the squad. Nevertheless this didn't mean that he would accept anything less than complete professionalism and responsibility from the players.

As had happened at Académica, the manager's new methods left everyone extremely pleased, and immediately many favourable comments were to be heard with various players describing his practices as "very dynamic and intense", "marked by the originality of the exercises that the manager draws on the pitch". As for the manager, he was "young, but has very good working methods", and it was easy to tell "that he is a very attentive and approachable manager, who tries to speak to us a lot, and strives to understand every detail about us". Even Raul Meireles, who had the opportunity of working with Villas-Boas just before leaving for Liverpool, later confided: "I worked with André for a month at FC Porto and he has a style like (José Mourinho). The practices are excellent, there is more variety and we practice with the ball a lot, which makes the work enjoyable. Everybody knows, if you practice well, you play well."

His dedication and commitment to work also impressed those who had the opportunity to follow him more closely. Citing as an example the pre-season training in Marienfeld, Germany, a source close to the team told us that Villas-Boas started the day early in the morning (8 am) and always worked until rather late (11 pm). Let's say that he was the first to wake up, and the last to get to bed.

He started his working day by having a meeting with the technical team. The objective was to finalise the last details for the two training sessions of the day. This was followed by breakfast, where he not only ate, but also caught up on reading the papers.

He would get to the pitch half an hour before practice time (which usually took place at 10 am) so as to have time to confirm that everything was set up according to plan. This was followed by the practice itself, which lasted approximately an hour and a half and was very intense. He often stepped in to guide, correct and encourage the players.

Lunch was at 1 pm, followed by a short break. At around 3 pm, there was another meeting, this time with all the staff, to take stock of the situation with regards to the squad, taking various aspects into account, such as the players' medical condition, for example. Then, he would once again head for the pitch half an hour before the afternoon practice (5 pm), which, like the morning session, was very lively and intense. The day would end with dinner (8 pm), followed by the third and final meeting of the day for a detailed analysis of the work carried out that day and also to thoroughly prepare the next day's work for the squad.

Whether on the training ground or off it, André Villas-Boas is permanently obsessed with his work. He is, without a doubt, a workaholic in the broadest sense of the word.

A GOALKEEPER, A CAPTAIN

On 13 March 2010, in a match in Coimbra, the Porto captain Mariano González suffered a serious injury that would see him oout of action for several months. He had ruptured ligaments, and it would be at least six months before his return. Though this was during the time when the team was still being coached by Jesualdo Ferreira, this situation, this misfortune for the Dragons' "ugly duckling" ended up having an impact the following season. Mariano continued to be one of the captains following the arrival of André Villas-Boas, but his absence from the pitch forced the new coach to select another captain, given that Bruno Alves and Raul Meireles had left the club.

It was a surprise to many that he chose the Brazilian goalkeeper Helton, who took on the role of first captain from among a group of four that also included Falcao, Hulk and, of course, the absent Mariano. The Argentinian remained close to the group and could always count on the full support of his companions. He was known as the player who created the best atmosphere and Jesualdo Ferreira had relied on him a great deal, even against the wishes of many Porto fans. He had seen Mariano as the player who put most effort into maintaining a positive atmosphere. And the group liked him.

André Villas-Boas was aware of all this. Mariano's absence had a real possibility of disrupting the dressing room, but by choosing Helton as captain – another player who was also well-liked by the whole group – AVB had resolved it.

The Brazilian's performance in the previous season had been very uneven and perhaps deserving of the booing of the fans and the various negative comments it had received. And so the decision that Villas-Boas took was a surprise to many – but his gamble on Helton paid off. The Porto fans soon began to see a new goalkeeper – one who was more motivated, more responsible, and with enough character to show wisdom and sensitivity in difficult times. His performance was greatly improved and he once again showed the many qualities that had originally led FC Porto to sign him from Leiria.

There and then, André Villas-Boas gained a goalkeeper and a strengthened group. He also managed to disprove a point that had always been made by the former FC Porto coach, Co Adriaanse, about who should be captain during a football match.

In years gone by, at the start of a difficult season for Jorge Costa, who ended up leaving Porto for Liége, Vítor Baía had been given the captain's armband. Later, the Dutch coach had stripped him of it, arguing that a goalkeeper could not be captain. The captain had to be an outfield player. Over time this was a view that had became almost set in stone, yet André Villas-Boas now did away with it.

Helton had, coincidentally, taken over from the legendary Baía in 2006 when Co Adriaanse had been manager. He became a captain in the style of the former Porto captains, and once said that "it is an easy task, even for a goalkeeper, when you're the captain of a disciplined group that enjoys playing football."

The young manager had made the right decision. He had gained a goalkeeper, a team and a captain.

THE BAD SIDE OF WINNERS

André Villas-Boas has that bad side of winners: he hates criticism and critics. He proved this early on during FC Porto's pre-season, with reactions very similar to those of José Mourinho. Despite trying to distance himself from Mourinho on the day he was presented as the Dragons' new manager, the truth is that he has always been very similar to the Special One, at least in the way that he reacts to criticism.

It was the beginning of August 2010 and the Paris Tournament was underway, the last one before the official start of the season. FC Porto had played badly in both matches against Paris Saint-Germain and Bordeaux. A huge disappointment in two crucial tests. Up until then – and despite consecutive wins over Trabzonspor (1-0), Ajax (1-0) and Sampdoria (2-1) – the team still hadn't won over the more sceptical fans and critics.

The Paris Tournament saw a slow, lethargic FC Porto that was easily dominated, though it was also possible to spot good points, such as some of the attacking play later highlighted by the press. But we were left with the feeling that there was a long road ahead. Falcao was also targeted by the reporters for not scoring goals, having previosuly had a fantastic debut season with Ferreira.

André emerged in front of the press, responding to the criticism rather harshly and insinuating ignorance on the part of those who were responsible for such analysis.

Only one week later, FC Porto won the Portuguese Super Cup in a surprising, well-deserved and brilliant display. At the press conference that followed, Villas-Boas immediately attacked those who had had bad things to say about the FC Porto that had played in Paris. In this moment of great victory, Villas-Boas wanted to take advantage of all the media attention to get back at those who, in his opinion, had misread what had happened in Paris.

The criticism that had been levelled at him had seemed to confirm the view of those who had said that Villas-Boas was too young to head a team such as Porto. This view held was that more experience was needed, particularly as the club had not won the League, something which had become most unusual over the last decade. The criticism bothered André who would nevertheless go on to enjoy a most victorious season. However, whenever the opportunity presented itself, he could not help himself from talking about the Paris Tournament and about those people who had got it all wrong.

A VIDEO THAT CHANGED A SEASON

Preparation for the first official match of the season – the Super Cup against Benfica on 7 August – started on the very first working day of 2 July, when André Villas-Boas first met the squad.

Benfica were an enemy to be shot down: the opponent that no Porto fan would ever want to see winning anything, had – according to most of the commentators – started a new cycle in Portuguese football by breaking away from the Dragons' domination. In addition to winning the 2009-10 Portuguese League, they had also had a pre-season full of trophies and goals galore. Exactly the same as the previous pre-season, which had propelled the team towards the title. At the same time, Benfica's manager, Jorge Jesus was being referred to as *Special Two*, and fuelled by his now-famous self-conviction he had recently stated live on television that it was most unlikely that Benfica would not yet again clinch the title. Furthermore, the last time both teams had met in a final, Benfica had calmly "demolished" FC Porto in a resounding 3-0 win. That had happened at the Algarve Stadium in March 2010 in the League Cup Final.

But on his first day with his team, on 2 July, André Villas-Boas immediately surprised his players. There are many ways to motivate and drive a team forward, and after some thought the new manager at FC Porto had an idea that naturally had a strong psychological effect on the entire group. While he was speaking to the players for the first time, in a room at the Olival training ground, a film was projected behind him, showing the Benfica players celebrating the 2009-10 victory. It wasn't necessary to say very much about the matter. The players immediately understood what the coach was after. Those images could not be repeated in the season that was about to begin.

Such compilation videos were usually just research projects carried out by assistant coach, Pedro Emanuel, and Acácio

Valentim, team manager of the club's principal squad. But that particular video was screened at all of Villas-Boas's pre-season talks. If a picture is worth a thousand words, then those images represented far more words than a thousand talks put together! The objective of the pre-season is to prepare the team, promote greater knowledge among everyone, internalise the manager's ideas and practise them in every match and training session. That was the message conveyed by Villas-Boas.

While the Benfica team were living off praise and planning another dream season, the Porto players would watch that video of the Benfica celebrations, enriched here and there with statements from the winning players that would, in some way, dent the pride of the Porto players.

Those images made their way into the players' sub-conscious, and that is why it was said that FC Porto carried out a match of revolt at the Super Cup. A revolt on the field that silenced the harshest of critics and, more importantly, left a mark on Jorge Jesus's Benfica team. That too was the objective.

Winning the Super Cup on 7 August 2010 was the direct result of an appetite refined by the desire for revenge. The objective was to put an end to Benfica's celebrations, which had extended into the pre-season. And it had been attained. Jorge Jesus acknowledged that Porto fully deserved to win by 2-0: "They were more effective than Benfica and are worthy winners". On the other hand, Villas-Boas explained that "it was the cry of revolt that FC Porto had to give. There was inspiration and a feeling of responsibility, as there had been the year before when Benfica had dared to think they would be champions where they shouldn't have (at the Dragon Stadium), and all of this led the Porto team to transcend themselves."

Later, at the press conference before the first match of the Portuguese League, Villas-Boas returned to the theme of motivation in connection with the resounding Super Cup win, and was even more explicit: "You can never overlook the factors of transcendence and motivation. There are, perhaps, some coaches who exacerbate the tactical work because it suits them and it also entails a certain type of promotion (an allusion to Jorge Jesus), but I always knew that the motivational factor would influence the players' performance and I advised them of this. When you add this motivational factor to a well-organised team, which has fully taken in the message, then you get great sporting performance. So, before the Super Cup match I spoke about the motivational factor, which to me matters a great deal." And indeed it did.

However, in that match, which allowed André Villas-Boas to become the second youngest coach ever to have won a title in Portugal, the Porto manager also showed that he was tactically very strong. This could be seen, for example, in the defensive positioning of Falcao, which cancelled out David Luiz's passing moves, forcing Luisão (the other Benfica centre-back, who's weaker with the ball at his feet) to start the build-up from Benfica's back line; or in the way that he instructed João Moutinho to cover Fábio Coentrão's upfield runs, which were crucial to Benfica's style of play; and also the way in which he put together a team which could control, almost entirely, the movements of the pairing of Aimar and Saviola, which had been a decisive factor in Benfica winning the championship.

FC Porto used the same tactical formation as in the previous season, 4-3-3, but it was much more flexible and greater emphasis was given to holding the ball. The midfield anchor was not limited to his defensive role, and from the midfield up the orders were to cause imbalances by constantly moving and switching positions. The team never kept still – a bit like their manager in fact – pressing right outside the Benfica penalty area. They applied a veritable "stranglehold" technique, and in the end the 2-0 result was flattering to the Reds from Lisbon.

In short, this was a completely new way of playing, for the better, and resorting to only one new player – the former Sporting midfielder, João Moutinho. This was seen as immediately revealing the sheer quality of the work being carried out by that young and inexperienced manager.

André Villas-Boas continued to use the video of Benfica the champions well after the Super Cup. Later, when FC Porto had a nine-point lead in the championship, he changed tack, and showed other motivational films: from screening compliments on a good performance to simply playing back the team's finest moments. The Benfica video was now left behind; its director had done a perfect job!

A NEW WAY OF COMMUNICATING

Among the various innovations that he implemented on his arrival at the club, André Villas-Boas instituted a new and particular way of dealing with the media: he decided not to grant anybody exclusive interviews. He would be at the disposal of all reporters only at the traditional press conferences.

Never before had an FC Porto manager taken control of the media in this way, and he kept to this decision for the entire season. At the press conferences, he answered all questions put to him in a sometimes provocative, but confident manner. He would stay for however long it took to answer everybody, he confronted reporters whenever necessary, and almost placed himself as if he were "on the other side" as he always addressed new issues. He even gave a few "lessons", established interesting dialogues, and always "supplied" a headline for the front pages. No reporter would leave Olival without a story to tell.

As far as we know, he rarely sought advice about what he was planning to say and, in a club where communication is closely controlled, that was frowned upon by those surrounding him. But as he heaped success upon success, he also started earning the right to talk about whatever he pleased.

At a certain point, he felt that his comments were not being accurately interpreted by reporters, or at least by some of them – "sometimes, sentences of mine are taken out of context or cut, and then appear the next day in newspaper articles or in a headline" – and so he decided that the press conferences would be recorded and then made available on the FC Porto site. More originality.

Fastidious about times and schedules, he was rarely ever late for press conferences. And on perhaps the only occasion that this happened, when he arrived at 1 pm for a conference that was scheduled for 12:30 pm, he resolved the matter with a statement that cracked everyone up, even the most annoyed amongst them: "I know that I've messed up your lunch plans… lunch will be on me."

While André Villas-Boas was available for lengthy conversations with reporters and no question was left unanswered, the manager at Benfica – as a result of the club's communication policy – only answered questions put forward by Benfica's official channel. Villas-Boas managed to make the most of this situation, and when his rival stated, "We know we are going to be champions again. We're going to be double-champions!" he promptly responded somewhat provocatively: "How many reporters did he say that to? Jorge Jesus's press conferences are monologues because they're granted exclusively to the club's channel. So, it's very easy to get your message across when there are no competing ideas and no other issues come up."

The so-called mind games, particularly in disputes with the Benfica manager, became a constant throughout the entire season. But when Jorge Jesus started coming under fire from within his own club, André Villas-Boas was quick to publicly defend him. "I have to come out in defence of someone who has given everything to a club, someone who has revolutionised a club and transformed its football, and who is now being treated like someone who has to be punished and penalised. It is shocking to see what is happening to a fellow professional, who has gone from "best" to "beast" in three short months – something that could happen to me," he stated with great sincerity.

By now, more and more foreign reporters were attending the press conferences, as they wanted to meet the man who was smashing anything and everything in FC Porto's path. This was even more so when, as a result of his success, his name began to be linked to various other leading European clubs, such as Juventus, Inter, Atlético Madrid, Chelsea, Liverpool and Roma. However not even the presence of these foreign reporters changed the way the young manager continued to answer all the questions he was asked. Even the most absurd, for instance, when he was asked whether it was true that Juventus had sent two represntatives to Porto to observe him. "Since when does a club send their people to scout a coach? It's absurd to say they're coming to observe me. During a match, a coach does little more than walk his suit alongside the bench and run a little from time to time."

At press conferences, André Villas-Boas always played on the attack, but in a most controlled manner. Just as his team were doing on the pitch.

"WE'RE IN THE EUROPA LEAGUE TO WIN"

André Villas-Boas's debut in top European football took place on 19 August 2010, in Genk, Belgium, against the local team. At the traditional press conference on the eve of the match, he promptly stated that "we're in the Europa League to win". Even taking into account that FC Porto were used to participating in the Champions League, the statement once more clearly demonstrated that Villas-Boas, despite usually being very reserved and balanced in what he says, likes to take risks. The statement was made before the match, measuring his words, and without worrying that he would have to bear the weight of that announcement for the entire competition.

On the day of the match, the Brazilian player Hulk, received some very sad news. One of his nieces, aged one and a half and the daughter of one of his sisters, had drowned in a pool at her home. Hulk was well on his way to an extraordinary season and was an important player for that match, but Villas-Boas didn't think twice. Setting aside all other interests, he arranged that FC Porto's support services would provide the player with everything that he needed to leave for Brazil immediately, via Porto, where he joined his wife and children. Nor did AVB want anyone to book a return ticket, letting it be known that the player should only return when he felt fully recovered emotionally. He lost a player for that important match, but he gained a footballer and a supporter for life.

The Brazilian was grateful. He returned home to be close to his sister and help her deal with the pain of her daughter's death. He returned to Porto four days later. Naturally, he received a great deal of attention from his fellow players and support from the club's directors – especially from the technical team who were concerned, above all, with the psychological side of the player as he had been through four days of intense pain. In fact, in Genk, in a clear demonstration of team spirit, his colleagues had dedicated their win to him, and Falcao had even displayed his shirt after they'd scored their first goal at the Cristal Arena.

The Brazilian player came back, and what a come back! It was motivation fuelled by the saddest of reasons. Hulk, who had missed the match against Genk in Belgium, and then another against Beira-Mar at the Dragon Stadium, came back for the second leg match against the Belgians and scored three of Porto's four goals in their 4-2 win.

André Villas-Boas, sticking to his principle of looking at the man first and then the player, was delighted with Hulk's three goals, but added that "he needs to experience moments of happiness after having gone through such deep sorrow. Mourning takes its time and we will respect that mourning". And Hulk once again came back at full strength on the pitch: he scored another two goals in FC Porto's victory (2-0) over Rio Ave in Vila do Conde!

The whole team were pleased with their manager's response. It had come about because of the saddest of circumstances, but now the players knew without a doubt that they also had a friend in André Villas-Boas.

HULK'S "HEARTBURN"

Hulk is the most valuable player on FC Porto's squad. He has a release payment clause set at a staggering 100 million Euros and Pinto da Costa has said that he would not exchange him for Cristiano Ronaldo, were that proposal ever to be put forward. Once again he became the focus of Villas-Boas's attention a short time later. Only this time, for poor professional reasons.

Hulk was unhappy after being substituted in Sofia in a match against CSKA, particularly as he had also been substituted in a home match against Rapid Vienna (both matches were part of the group phase in the Europa League). The television pictures didn't lie and clearly showed his annoyance. However, the Brazilian striker's agent was quick to explain that everything had been sorted out with Villas-Boas at the end of the match. And, indeed, so it was.

Contrary to what you would expect or imagine, Villas-Boas never had private conversations with players when they were upset. He always spoke to them face to face, but within the group. His message was: "What matters here is the group, the club, and not this or that player in particular." With this attitude, which has much to recommend it, he had clearly taken a stand. He was a young manager of a young squad and would never tolerate any lack of respect, whether it took place in training or during a match.

When asked if he was bothered by Hulk's obvious discontent, he simply answered, "No, absolutely not, as long as nobody hits me."

And he took advantage of this opportunity to explain why he had substituted the Brazilian which had nothing to do with "effort management" given that he'd made the substitutions in the Sofia match because: "the nature of the game was changing and we needed more rest and calmness with the ball, to keep the match more in the attacking midfield, as we were failing to control the ball in the last third of the field. I sent Varela on because he doesn't break away as much as Hulk or Walter, and because he holds the ball more, and passes it more with the midfielders." And then he brought the matter to an end by conveying to the outside world what had already been said inside: "No player will ever be allowed to fulfil individual ambitions rather than collective ones."

Little by little, the players realised that it wasn't worth getting upset. The results took care of the rest, because when a team wins, everything becomes much easier and those who don't play lose the will to show their displeasure. Ruben Micael, for example, a promising young player arrived at Porto after a battle with Sporting to sign him. He promptly lost his place to the newly-arrived João Moutinho. There was also no other space for him in Villas-Boas's midfield, as at the same time the Argentine, Belluschi, had begun to show just how good he could be. Even though he was usually a reserve player, Micael was nevertheless still called up for the Portuguese national side by manager Paulo Bento. In his debut he scored Portugal's two winning goals (2-0) in a friendly against Finland. At the end of the match he expressed his disappointment at being a reserve at Porto. But little good did it do him.

In this era of social networks, Fredy Guarín, sought solace on Twitter. After a spectacular goal against Seville in the Europa League (which would prove crucial in the knock-out round), and another great goal in Moscow, also in the Europa League, the player tweeted the following: "I don't know what else to do to be an automatic choice at FC Porto." This outburst was justified and resulted from yet another season of not being a first choice, as the same had happened with Jesualdo Ferreira. As always, Villas-Boas spoke at the press conference and made his position very clear when he said that "those who I feel should play, will play." Full stop. We do not know who won this battle, but the truth is that Guarín went on to play quality football and finished the season in tremendous form, and was for many one of the most important players in André Villas-Boas's FC Porto.

Another case that marked the season was that of striker Walter, one of the signings for the 2010-11 season. The Brazilian would only play for a few minutes, but he scored goals – which is after all what is required of a player in that position. But at a certain point, even when Falcao was injured, Walter stopped being an option for Villas-Boas, who wouldn't even put him on the substitute's bench. The manager was therefore forced to have Hulk spearhead the attack, and Walter continued not to make it into the team. There was a great deal of speculation about ill-advised behaviour in the player's private life, but André Villas-Boas based his decision solely on what he saw of a player's attitude on the pitch, especially during training. He was extremely demanding during the training sessions, and wanted all the players to put as much effort into them as if they were playing a real match. He also wanted them to work intensely on the game plan he had chosen, which in the case of strikers involved exerting great pressure on the opponent's defence. From Villas-Boas's point of view, Walter wasn't following his instructions regarding the team's tactical strategy, especially in terms of constant pressing, and so he therefore stopped relying on him. However, that didn't stop the manager from defending the player when allegations arose that Walter spent too many nights partying in Porto. He denied the stories, turning on whoever had started circulating the rumours.

When the striker said that he might return to Brazil, the manager commented: "Walter's outburst is natural. We want him to succeed. He knows what message I conveyed, because I did so in front of all his team mates." Once again confirming that André Villas-Boas likes to resolve things face to face and in front of the entire team. An effective and instructive way of overcoming any possible sources of discontent.

I, A POOR SINNER, CONFESS MYSELF

A convincing, decisive and motivating victory in the first official match of the 2010-11 season set FC Porto on a truly astounding start to the season, with win after win and record upon record.

But after eleven consecutive wins in various competitions, including six wins in the League, Porto ran into their first hitch. It happened at the D. Afonso Henriques Stadium, in Guimarães, on the seventh match day in a game that was controversial, not because of what actually took place, but more so because of the reaction of the Porto fans, and in particular the reaction of André Villas-Boas.

FC Porto didn't play particularly well, and drew 1-1. Halfway through the match their full-back, Fucile, was red-carded after an extremely dangerous tackle on the Moroccan, Faouzi. It happened right in front of the Dragons' bench. The young manager jumped onto the pitch, and headed towards the referee, Carlos Xistra, who sent him off as a result of his protests.

In the post-match press conference, Villas-Boas was still not himself. He surprised all the reporters as he explained that his reaction was because of a foul by Alex on Ruben Michael for which the referee should have given Porto a penalty. It was just moments before the incident that had led to Fucile being sent off.

As it happened, no one had seen any reason for a penalty. Villas-Boas was incredibly critical of the referee, even accusing him of playing a decisive role in the outcome of the match (which ended 1-1, even though Porto had been winning 1-0 at the time of the incident). "There was a clear error that changed the direction of the match," he stated.

However, Villas-Boas belief that it was a penalty was based on information he had received from the club's press officer, Rui Cerqueira, who in turn had based his response on a message from a friend. Unreliable information, therefore, but Villas-Boas had trusted it, which is perhaps something that tends to happen in these circumstances.

This happened on 4 October 2010. A day later, TVI – the channel that had broadcast the match live – screened the images once more and proved that there had been no reason to give a penalty after all. Villas-Boas once again surprised everyone by putting out a statement on FC Porto's website in which he acknowledged that it hadn't been a penalty, and apologised for his over-reaction during the match as well as his post-match comments. "We have confirmed that there really was no reason to have been awarded a penalty. In relation to that, the criticism is unfounded and unfair," read the statement.

An act of contrition, a *mea culpa* that took the critics by surprise. Villas-Boas had already been accused of being a bad loser and of wavering psychologically at the first sign of adversity. Nevertheless, this was also a risky act, very uncommon in Portuguese football. It ended up having a positive effect at two levels: firstly, AVB learnt to be more careful with his remarks (so much so, that during the season he rarely commented on any controversial play without first viewing it); secondly, the manager gained sympathy, even from unlikely quarters, although he didn't escape some criticism. It was, nevertheless, an extremely surprising action from someone who was beginning to make an impression on Portuguese football.

OPERA

Life was going well for André Villas-Boas.

The young Porto manager had many reasons to be happy: he had celebrated a year as manager, now with one of Portugal's "big" clubs (his FC Porto), his second daughter was born, he turned 33 (on 17 October) and the team, which grew from match to match, was not only winning but doing so with quality performances. Both in Portugal and in Europe.

But after the resounding win in the August Super Cup, the second clash of the season against Benfica was coming up. After a shaky start in the League with three defeats in four matches, Benfica were now on a winning streak and were only a scant seven points behind Porto. The match, which would be played at the Dragon Stadium, was vitally important to Benfica. If they won, they could potentially place a question mark over FC Porto's successful path towards the league title.

As he had done in the first match of the season, André Villas-Boas once again placed emphasis on motivation and the importance of the group. He recalled an incident from the previous season in which Hulk and Sapunaru had allegedly assaulted a steward in the players' tunnel at the Benfica Stadium, and had been suspended for a few months as a result. Porto insisted this had been an ambush of sorts, set up by Benfica in order to "get rid of" the best Porto player.

"FC Porto will be a team in a permanent state of revolt as a result of the targets it did not achieve last season and the injustice suffered by two of its players," was how André Villas-Boas referred to the game in the pre-match press conference. And he continued in the same vein, stating that he believed "in the importance of a good team talk, despite the way football today can seem to be so tactical. It suits many people to emphasise this aspect so as to disguise weaknesses. Having human qualities is also very important. I believe in the values of transcendence, in the strength of the dressing room. In the Super Cup match there was a cry of revolt, and that cry continues, for all the injustices committed in the previous season."

Whenever André Villas-Boas emphasised the opinion that some gave particular importance to the tactical approach so as to conceal various weaknesses, he was referring indirectly to Jorge Jesus, who was then Benfica manager. Jesus considered himself a professor of tactics, though he was regarded by others as someone with an old-school dressing room leadership style, one which can be very taxing on the players.

Interestingly enough, it was the tactical plan for the match that generated much speculation. How would Jorge Jesus set up his team so as to cancel out the powerful Hulk? Would he have David Luiz, the best centre-back in the championship, playing at left-back, and move Fábio Coentrão, the best left-back, up to the midfield? In the previous season, during a UEFA Cup match, he had tried this in Liverpool with disastrous results: 4-1 in favour of the Reds, as Benfica bowed out of the competition at quarter-final stage.

FC Porto's manager was unconcerned and said he was ready for a possible change to his opponent's defensive organisation: "I don't know if David Luiz will play left-back. If that happens, then things will change. I've already spoken to the players about this and we will be ready."

Benfica did, in fact, go with David Luiz at left-back and Fábio Coentrão further upfield than usual. Once again the result was catastrophic. Half an hour into the match Porto were already ahead by 3-0. André Villas-Boas had said he was ready for Benfica's changes, and apparently he really was: the three goals originated from exactly that part of the pitch. FC Porto didn't slow the pace and the final result was a famous 5-0 victory, the result of an extraordinary performance.

Talking about David Luiz playing left-back, Villas-Boas said at the end of the match: "Without being critical, it is important to note that our opponents altered the dynamics with that change. Perhaps they gambled too highly on a duel and believed that this duel could fix all the problems, but what happened was exactly the opposite. A match is a duel between two organisations, and not between two individual forces." And going back once again to the subject of revolt, he added: "On the pitch, we gave our cry of revolt, which related back to the events of last year, and we have managed an historic result against the national champions."

With this win, FC Porto were now ten points ahead of Benfica in second place, and most observers viewed the league title race as over. Yet it was still only the first half of November. Villas-Boas, however, was not swept away by the general euphoria, and he explained why: "I had a similar experience with José Mourinho at Chelsea, when we were 12 points ahead of Manchester United. We were 12 points ahead but we never stopped feeling the pressure."

Mourinho (always Mourinho!) had said that he thought that winning the Portuguese League was not a difficult task. Many interpreted this statement as a way of devaluing the work that André Villas-Boas was carrying out. And the FC Porto manager himself felt the need to defend himself, saying that he disagreed entirely and that "there are no easy championships to win. It wasn't easy for us to win at Inter; it wasn't easy for Mourinho to bring the title back to Chelsea after fifty years. I think it's ridiculous to say that." But the truth of the matter is that Mourinho had already said exactly the same thing in November 2004, that is, a long time before André Villas-Boas had even dreamt of being FC Porto's manager: "It is harder in England. In the two seasons at FC Porto it was rather easy to win the League."

At the end of December, FC Porto still remained unbeaten, with 23 wins in 26 official matches, having scored 64 goals and only conceded 12. And it was at this time that Pinto da Costa announced the renewal of Villas-Boas's contract, which would run until the end of the 2012-13 season. He explained that that was "the only way to show confidence in the manager" and added that he hoped it would be "the first of many contract renewals with André Villas-Boas".

Life continued to go well for André Villas-Boas.

STEP BY STEP

In companies, targets are set and monitored on a monthly basis, and sometimes on a weekly or even daily basis, so that the overall target can be reached at the end of the year. André Villas-Boas followed the same philosophy in his first season at FC Porto: he kept giving the squad small targets, one after the other, in order to achieve the main targets or even surpass them.

Many asked how it was possible for a team to always have such high levels of motivation, and to always show such a desire to win even when the outcome of a match was of almost negligible importance. By parcelling up their objectives, André Villas-Boas always kept the players under pressure, but a healthy pressure, which turned into motivation.

In August, at the end of the second match day and after a 3-0 home win over Beira-Mar, André Villas-Boas already noted: "The first target was to be top of the table," and then added that there was "a strong feeling, in the changing room, of target achieved." Had FC Porto already won something? No, by the second match day nothing had yet been won, but the team had started the League programme without making things easier for anyone. They had won their first two matches and had left Benfica, a target to be shot down, six points behind!

Before Christmas, for instance, when Porto were already comfortably heading the championship, the objective set was to win the four matches to be played before the players set off on their Christmas holidays. In order to maintain the distance between them and their opponents. Villas-Boas's messages were first transmitted to his team, and then made public in press conferences to ensure they did not deviate from them in any way.

Before the last of these four matches, in Paços de Ferreira, the president of the local team made the statement that FC Porto's winning streak would come to an end there. Villas-Boas thanked him for his help: "The ideal atmosphere for the game has been created. I'm thankful for what the president of Paços has said as this has heightened our motivation. We would have been motivated in any case, but if there were any chance of being distracted by the holidays, Christmas and shopping, those words ensured it would not happen." And FC Porto headed towards Christmas with another four victories in the bag. In Paços de Ferreira they won by 3-0.

Someone who did not seem to understand this philosophy very well was Benfica manager, Jorge Jesus. In response to a declaration by Villas-Boas, who had said that Benfica were down 10-1 in their last three clashes against FC Porto (3-1 at the end of the 2009-10 season with Jesualdo Ferreira, 2-0 in the Super Cup and 5-0 in the League with Villas-Boas), Jorge Jesus said that Benfica did their 'accounting' on the basis of "titles won and not on matches. Winning matches is important but, in the end, it's the titles that count." We can safely assume that this reply from Jesus became yet another motivational tool that could and would be used by André Villas-Boas.

As a matter of fact, the FC Porto manager always paid a great deal of attention to what his rivals said, especially Benfica, so that he could make the most of those statements to further motivate his own group. "What they say are *fait-divers*. They're comments we put up on the board and then look at during the week," he explained.

The philosophy of setting sub-goals had another fundamental advantage: it forced the team to always look ahead and forget the euphoria that victories always bring. That is, this target-setting stopped the team from resting on its laurels in terms of the lead they had, the competitions they had already qualified for, or even the titles they had won. Once one target was reached, another was on the immediate horizon.

A constant concern of Villas-Boas throughout the season was to bring the fans and the team back down to earth after each and every success. Immediately after winning the Super Cup, he set the tone: "It is important for the team not to let up in the light of the many, recent compliments." After the remarkable 5-0 win over Benfica, a win which had lifted the team's spirit to new heights, he found it necessary to control his players' jubilation by saying that the score was indeed the result of an extraordinary performance, but that this was an abnormal result, one of those that are few and far between. At the beginning of the second half of the season, he was once again very clear about the message he wanted to transmit: "We've had five great months, but it's the next five months that are crucial."

At this stage, people had already stopped talking about André Villas-Boas as a young and inexperienced manager, and had started writing about the revelation of a great football manager, a new success story, along the lines of José Mourinho.

Further ahead in the season than expected, and well on his way to winning the title, AVB set another goal: for Porto to be made champions at the stadium of their greatest rival. But to be able to pull this off, the team would have to win five consecutive matches. The audacity of these statements seemed to bother his Lisbon rivals a great deal, and public opinion began to focus on Villas-Boas's haughty arrogance. Deep down, though, everyone knew that it was possible. Villas-Boas's idea (to become champions upon their visit to the Luz Stadium) disturbed Benfica to such an extent that the Dragons did indeed go on to clinch the League title in that very match. The 2-1 win went down very well, though the players and the rest of the technical team had to celebrate in the dark as someone had decided to switch off the stadium lights and turn on the sprinkler system as soon as the Porto fans and team began to celebrate.

That attempt to dampen spirits failed and instead the blackout at Luz would provide new phrases of encouragement for the FC Porto players. In the darkness, you can imagine that André would have been smiling. Nobody had stopped celebrating and now they had found something else to use as another motivational target.

Having already won the League, which was the main target for the season, other goals were immediately established for the remainder of the competition: to be undefeated champions, to set a new points record of goals scored and conceded. The team also had other objectives to achieve up until the end of the season, namely winning the Europa League and the Portuguese Cup, but that didn't stop Villas-Boas from setting his players new challenges. And the players willingly took them on. As well as being the third youngest coach ever to win a Portuguese championship, at 33 years of age, the Porto manager also went on to win the League undefeated, something that until then only Jimmy Hagan's [27] Benfica could pride itself on.

At the beginning of the season, sitting in his "dream seat", Villas-Boas had said what one naturally says upon arriving at a club with the ambitions of FC Porto: that they were in every competition to win. Only the League Cup slipped through their fingers. However, even today, there are those who say that that elimination, decided on the day of their first defeat, and at the Dragon Stadium, in a match against Nacional da Madeira after the Christmas holidays, was the best outcome one could have asked for. Contrary to what usually happens, the team didn't become despondent at

---

27. *Jimmy Hagan (1918-1998) played for Derby County (1935-1938) and Sheffield United (1938-1958), and once for England. He arrived in Portugal in 1970 to manage Benfica. In three seasons with the club he won three championships and a Portuguese Cup. In 1972-73, leading a team in which Eusébio ruled, he won the championship unde-feated (28 wins and two draws, scoring an unbelievable 101 goals). He left Benfica at the start of the 1973-74 season, after problems with the club's Board for not having called up Humberto Coelho and Toni, two of the most important players on the squad, for Eusébio's testimonial match.*

having missed that target; instead they set off with increased ambition to win everything else that was left.

But the first loss of the season, on the twenty-seventh match, revealed an André Villas-Boas full of fair play. He calmly explained that defeat is also a part of football and that it can appear at any given moment. And he also emphasised the fact that it is not "one loss that will call everything into question. You do not penalise a team that has performed well over the months." The Porto fans appreciated his stand, and Rui Moreira, president of the Porto Commercial Association and elected Golden Dragon[28] in 2010 as "Member of the Year", even wrote that we were "left with the certainty that there was a leader on the bench, who admits defeat, who doesn't look for easy excuses, who doesn't 'burn' his players and who doesn't lose the fair play he'd already shown when winning." And the team also responded in a positive way: in the following match at home, they thrashed Marítimo 4-1, and ended the first leg of the League with 13 wins and 2 draws, 36-6 in goals.

The other domestic cup to be won was the Portuguese Cup. FC Porto and Benfica met at the Dragon Stadium for the first leg of the semi-finals on 2 February. Surprisingly, Benfica won by 2-0 and were therefore technically ahead given that the second leg would be played at the Luz Stadium, and because of the tiebreaker system adopted by European competitions, where, in case of a draw, an away goal can count double. FC Porto, therefore, had a problem to get to grips with. They would have to overcome that disadvantage, which essentially meant they would have to score at least three goals in Lisbon. And immediately after that match at the Dragon Stadium, Villas-Boas promised he would fight to make it to the Portuguese Cup Final: "Take note, for us the match does not end here. It is a difficult task, but not unattainable." He accepted the

---

28. *The Golden Dragon is an annual award, attributed by FC Porto's Board to players, coaches, directors, employees and affiliates of the club who have distinguished them- selves throughout a season. A Golden Dragon is also awarded to a club member.*

result with good grace; he did not waver from his path, and kept to his target of winning by 3-0 at Benfica's Luz Stadium.

There followed a two-month wait for the second leg of the semi-final match, which took place on 20 April. But for the Porto players and fans it was well worth it. The Luz Stadium was euphoric, and in the changing room Villas-Boas made the most of the emotional atmosphere. In his talk he simply asked his players to do what they knew best, without any inhibitions. And he added: "Let's rewrite destiny." They did what he asked of them, and Benfica were no longer in the running for the Cup Final. The final score was 3-1 to FC Porto.

Step by step, all of the targets – except one, and perhaps the least important – were reached. André Villas-Boas later summarised it in a very simple and direct manner: "The team at FC Porto set step by step goals, motivation was ever-present and that is essential in modern football. That is all that happened this season."

TALKS

Many people think that the pre-match talk is a key component in the preparation leading up to a game. And it may well be, for a variety of different reasons, but the truth of the matter is that for modern coaches what is said to the players throughout the week is much more important. At a time when science has made its way into football – one need only look at the number of coaches with a degree in physical education whose more calculated and rational approach has taken the place of that of the empiricists – preparation for the match begins with the first training session of the week or, when teams are short on both time and space during those busier periods, two or three days before the match.

This is exactly the approach that André Villas-Boas adopted at FC Porto. He would begin preparing for the matches through short conversations with the players, addressing details related to the positioning of the team and the players themselves, and by talking about their opponents and their motivation, the surrounding atmosphere, etc. Greater care would be taken, for example, if they were up against opponents who seemed to be more motivated as a result of a series of recent wins. The young manager is someone who is particularly attentive, and that is worth a lot, especially when you are surrounded by a technical team that thinks along the same lines.

The preparation carried out in the days before a match meant that on the match day itself, it was not necessary to say very much at those pre-match talks. At FC Porto, André Villas-Boas usually spoke to the players twice on the day of a match. The first talk, at around lunch time, was more concerned with psychological issues. We have already mentioned the video of Benfica celebrating the League Title the previous season – the video that accompanied FC Porto on the first few match days of the season, and which the players were shown almost immediately after Villas-Boas had been appointed manager. In Dublin, when FC Porto played in the Europa League Final against SC Braga on 18 May, the film was completely different. The first talk of the day was accompanied by a video with snippets of Europa League matches, showing Porto's absolutely impeccable journey to the Final. The collection of images he screened in that meeting truly moved the players. And the message was very clear: those who had played so beautifully up until then could really do nothing else but win the Final. The players easily understood the message; the manager didn't need to say very much.

In an interview to the sports newspaper, *O Jogo*, the goalkeeper and captain, Helton, said that the "talk moved us a lot… it was marvellous. Spectacular. It made us think, reflect. When it's more of the same, for example, 'Let's go play to win', it doesn't have such a great effect on the players because we always hear that. That was different, he always adds something new, and that is spectacular."

Without wanting to reveal what André Villas-Boas had told the group, he did however say that the manager had said "many very good things. And when I say many, I'm not referring to the time taken, but to the content. He spoke to us at the hotel before we left for the stadium. We left there feeling even more confident that we were going to win, more confident about what we had to do to win. That confidence helped us a lot. It was a fantastic and unique moment."

And FC Porto once again lifted a European trophy, the fourth in their history: a European Champions Cup in 1987, a UEFA Cup in 2003, the Champions League in 2004 and then, in 2011, the Europa League.

"At the end of all the talks he gives, the players stop to think. You can be certain that there isn't a single talk that doesn't end this way." It was Helton, once again, who had said this in another interview to the same newspaper some months before.

MAGNIFICENT SECOND HALVES

The most exciting phase of the season was from March to May 2011, when FC Porto took everyone by storm and won the Portuguese League, the Europa League and the Portuguese Cup. During this phase, there were many games with a magnificent second half, in which the team completely turned the matches round and more than made up for a first half that hadn't gone as well as planned, or in which Porto were even down by a goal or more.

André Villas-Boas always sought to downplay his role during the half-time interval, never revealing if he had made changes in how the team were to play. This was in complete contrast to the players who would lavish praise on the manager's talks in the changing room before going back on the pitch.

"What he said to us at the half-time interval was very

important," said the Colombian, Guarín, after the extraordinary 5-1 win over Villarreal, in the first leg of the Europa League semi-final held at the Dragon Stadium. At half-time the score had been 1-0 in favour of the Spaniards. There were those who noticed a tactical shift – from 4-3-3 in the first half to 4-1-4-1 in the second – but the Porto manager denied it all: "There was no tactical change; I don't know where they got the 4-1-4-1 from." And, with his traditional modesty, he explained that "what changed in the second half was the effectiveness. I didn't say anything special… nothing of what I said was decisive in our turning the result round. A negative result followed by a "turn-around" doesn't mean that the manager is a master tactician."

In the match against Spartak Moscow, in the same competition and also at home, FC Porto went from a favourable, but by no means comfortable position at half-time (1-0) to a resounding 5-1 by the end of the game. What did he say to the players in the dressing room? "I asked for calmness and careful decision-making, because it's through that that you achieve the best way of playing." That's it? Yes, it is. André Villas-Boas trusted his players who, as a result of the work carried out during training, knew exactly what they had to do and, therefore, there was nothing else for him to add at half-time.

Then there was the second leg of the Portuguese Cup semi-final, when Porto were 0-0 at half-time yet needed to score three goals to guarantee their place in the final. "I told the players to keep calm. We kept to the initial message, which was not to stress out if the first goal was late in coming. In the first half, Benfica played containment football, without applying their characteristic speed, and that made us passive. We needed that touch of aggressiveness." In the end Porto won 3-1, turning the second leg match round in their favour (they had previously lost 0-2 at home) and the team reached the final. As always, Villas-Boas immediately looked to the future: "This win will barely be remembered if we don't win the trophy." In other words, no euphoria.

Apart from the spectacular performances and goals offered by the team, the magnificent second halves made it possible for André Villas-Boas to get some of the most worn out players on the squad to rest. The manager, who always focussed on his objectives, was never very keen on player rotation and made this clear throughout the season, as we will see below.

In fact, as early as October, when Porto had already qualified for the Europa League group phase, and were soon to receive Besiktas just before playing Benfica at the Dragon Stadium in a Portuguese League match, he stated: "Am I going to spare some players for the match against Besiktas because of the upcoming game against Benfica? No way. And for one simple reason: I never spare players." And spare players he did not.

Later in the season, FC Porto were to play Leiria. It was following a match in Moscow in the Europa League, which had required great effort, a long return trip, and had been played on a synthetic pitch against a difficult opponent (CSKA). Despite having a significant lead in the League, he ruled out any chance of sparing players so that they would not entertain the idea of taking things easy. "There doesn't have to be any relaxing or sparing of players. The players know all too well that the idea that everything is in the bag can be dangerous; I'm sure that there'll never be any danger of relaxing." In other words, a technical decision with psychological objectives. Here again is the issue of not separating out the various components of a coach's work, something that is so important to "tactical periodisation" and to the complexity theory, both of which were addressed earlier in this book.

And, after "demolishing" Spartak Moscow with a 5-1 win at the Dragon Stadium, he responded in much the same way when asked if there would be any player management for the second leg match: "No, not at all. Nobody views things as settled. The result is really comfortable, but we must stay alert."

However, the most extraordinary example was in the second leg match of the Europa League semi-finals against Villarreal. After once again having won 5-1 at home, he selected midfielder João Moutinho for the away leg at El Madrigal. Moutinho was one of their strongest and most important players, and if he had received a yellow card he wouldn't have been available to play in the Final. But, yet again, AVB was firm: "There is no possible management. The final will only exist for us if we are successful here in Villarreal." Case closed.

How then did André Villas-Boas resolve the issue of "effort management", which is so necessary to some of the more overworked players over a long season? Once more, it makes perfect sense to look at the analysis carried out by Luís Freitas Lobo: "When he makes changes to the team, he usually does so in midfield. The timing of the changes: between 60 and 75 minutes. He removes a winger from the attack and thereby makes a midfield quartet, intermediate base of the 4-4-2 and its variants (diamond shape or 1-3). In this way, he avoids the 'wear and tear' and tactical fatigue that the 4-3-3 may more easily cause to the team (and to the individual players), and he avoids speaking about 'tired players' or a 'worn out team'. The time he makes the change is also fully considered. At its best, the team begins to recover for the following match... in the previous match. The 4-4-2 clearly makes it possible to rest more with the ball (possession for possession's sake)."

4-3-3, BALL POSSESSION & HIGH PRESSURE

"I continue to say that all styles are good provided they lead to victory. I know what my style is, and what I like to put forward, which is a protagonist style of having the ball, knowing how to move it about and creating a greater number of goal opportunities. But there is no doubt in my mind that pragmatism and a result-geared mentality are firmly entrenched in Portugal. Often the solution to problems lies in set plays because in Portugal players aren't thought to be creative enough. I respect this opinion, but I disagree completely because the Portuguese player is creative by nature, and there have been many examples of this over the last 50 years. It is a fact that pragmatism leads to results and even to absolute success, but I defend this style of mine."

This extract appeared in the *Diário de Coimbra* and is, of course, a quote from André Villas-Boas. However, if you think that the remark was made recently then you are mistaken. It is from an interview he gave while still managing Académica. In fact, the young manager has always stuck to his principles of play, even when he was coaching the less ambitious club, whose key objective was to avoid relegation.

Even before he had joined FC Porto, André Villas-Boas had acknowledged that 4-3-3 was "cultural" in Portuguese football, and that he would never abdicate from that tactic, and that's what he did when he arrived at the club. The 4-3-3 that he implemented gained greater predominance once it was understood that he would set up a midfield trident with Fernando, a midfield anchor who usually provides support for the defenders, Moutinho, who had just arrived at Porto, and Belluschi, an Argentine international midfielder who hadn't enjoyed a successful season after arriving at the club in the Summer of 2009. Perhaps he hadn't expected this triangle to get an extremely important reinforcement: the Colombian Fredy Guarín.

Under Jesualdo Ferreira, Guarín had played an important role at the end of the previous season. With him playing as a type of defensive midfielder, FC Porto had been able to clean up what they had done wrong in the first third of the season, without Hulk. With Hulk back on the team and Guarín turning out to be a pleasant surprise, but in a scheme much closer to a 4-4-2, the Dragons made up ground and ended the season in great style, although they did not make it on time to enter the Champions League.

André thrilled the crowds with his 4-3-3 many times, but with a group of players that had learnt high pressing football. Falcao, who had once thanked Jesualdo for teaching him to play with his back to the goal, was the first defender of a team that was always ready to attack. In his talks, André never tired of repeating the word concentration. And it worked.

"Football is chaotic" is perhaps one of the most notable expressions proffered by Villas-Boas. In several press conferences, he was asked about which tactic he would use in this or that game. He always chose 4-3-3, but would also say that the players had the freedom to create. "There's no point in being rigid when it comes to tactics. Players have the freedom to be creative on the pitch, also because it might be necessary to change things during the match. I will never move away from this tactical system, but changes throughout the match may alter the system, though only when the occasion calls for it."

Is football chaotic? Of course it is – not least because it is brought to life through the inspiration of the players. That is what AVB has always sought to convey, although he has occasionally been misunderstood, with reporters sometimes misinterpreting his chosen formation as 4-4-2 rather than 4-3-3.

Nevertheless, like José Mourinho, Villas-Boas believes that a team must not lose its character because of its opponents. If the system of play is to be changed, it must never be done *because* of the opposing team. In other words, his team is always the most important, and never the team they are playing against. Even when some have pointed to tactical alterations the manager has supposedly implemented in the team – a good example being the apparent change from the first to second half in the previously mentioned home match against Villarreal – the Porto manager has publicly denied that anything has been changed, insisting that the team has remained consistent to his game plan.

Another very important characteristic advocated by André Villas-Boas relates to ball possession. Back when he was coaching Académica, most of the analysts would already draw attention to the team's capacity to hold onto the ball. At Porto this characteristic became even stronger, perhaps due to the greater quality of the players he had at his disposal. The team liked to take on the game via ball possession, a key characteristic of modern football, which is taken to extremes and to near perfection by Guardiola's Barcelona.

When it was noted that FC Porto scored few goals through set-plays, he replied that "the more goals we score by continuously attacking, the better for us. How many teams in Portugal settle their matches with set-plays – something which then results in an absolutely boring game? It's not our concern if teams are waiting to exploit that one moment, just because they don't have other options. It means that our football has enough quality to create opportunities and finish them off. It's a sign that what we do through an organised attack is good."

André Villas-Boas's FC Porto will be remembered as a team that favoured ball possession, that based its football on passing technique and on calm and forward-moving football.

Another aspect that received much praise throughout the season was the team's ability to press their opponent's far upfield, in a very aggressive manner. By means of excellent organisation and a strong positional sense, he avoided – in exemplary fashion – the usual tactical imbalances that happen when you lose the ball and attack turns into defence. And why? "It is rare to see an unbalanced FC Porto immediately after losing the ball. And when they recover it, they are immediately well positioned to continue playing. This happens because the more you reduce transition times, almost mixing them up within the formation, the more tactically balanced a team is on the pitch," explained Luís Freitas Lobo. In other words, step by step, or rather pass by pass, the team built up the game, something which would later allow it to be tactically very well balanced and positioned even after losing the ball, and so be able to immediately begin the work to recover it.

RECORD HOLDER

FC Porto's extraordinary performances throughout the 2010-11 season made it possible for André Villas-Boas to beat an endless number of international, national and club records. Added to that there have also been a host of equally impressive achievements. Let us take a look at some of the more significant numbers:

- Youngest-ever coach to win a UEFA competition, the 2010-11 Europa League, at the age of 33 years and 213 days, beating Gianluca Vialli, who won the Cup of Cups for Chelsea in 1998, aged 33 and 308 days, and Sven-Goran Eriksson, who won the UEFA Cup for IFK Göteborg in 1982, aged 34 and 102 days.

- The 11th coach in the history of European football to achieve a treble (domestic league, domestic cup and a European competition). At FC Porto, only Mourinho had managed such a feat (2002-03 season – Portuguese League, Portuguese Cup and UEFA Cup).

- The most expensive transfer ever for a football coach – 15 million Euros paid by Chelsea to FC Porto.

- First undefeated Portuguese coach – FC Porto ended the 2010-11 Portuguese League with an incredible 27 wins, 3 draws and no defeats. Porto scored 73 goals (2.43 per match) and only conceded 16 (0.53 per match).

- The most productive manager at FC Porto points-wise at the end of a championship: an average of 2.80 points per match. Next on this table is José Mourinho at 2.53 (2002-03), António Oliveira at 2.50 (1996-97) and Bobby Robson at 2.47 (1995-96).

- Winner with the greatest points difference in relation to the 2nd placed team – FC Porto were 21 points ahead of Benfica, and a staggering 36 points ahead of 3rd placed Sporting!

- FC Porto season with the highest number of official matches played: 58 (30 League, 7 Portuguese Cup, 17 Europa League, 3 League Cup and 1 Portuguese Super Cup). After this come the seasons 2000-01 with 56 matches (Fernando Santos) and 2003-04 with 55 matches (José Mourinho).

- Most victorious season ever – in all the competitions FC Porto participated in, they won 49 matches out of 58.

- Greatest goal scoring season ever – in all the competitions FC Porto participated in, they scored an impressive 145 goals, an average of 2.5 goals per match.

- Youngest-ever Porto manager to win a trophy – the Portuguese Super Cup at the start of the 2010-11 season, still aged 32.

- FC Porto manager with the highest number of European matches in a single season – a total of 17, all for the Europa League: two in the play offs, six in the group phase, eight in the qualifying round and lastly, the final.

- Greatest number of titles in a single season: four – equalling Tomislav Ivic, who in the 1987-88 season won the League, the Portuguese Cup, the European Super Cup (beating Ajax) and the Intercontinental Cup (beating Peñarol). However, André Villas-Boas's feat can be considered superior to that of

Ivic, as he won the European competition he played in.

- Most comfortable win in a Portuguese Cup Final – FC Porto beat Vitória de Guimarães 6-2 in the match that brought the season to a close.

- Greatest thrashing of Benfica ever for the championship, 5-0 in the match played at the Dragon Stadium.

Let us return to Luís Freitas Lobo. In an article entitled *"Being Special: Reason and Art"*, and after placing André Villas-Boas on a roll of football coaches he considered special (such as Herrera, Cruyff, Clough, Mourinho, Michels), he concluded: "Would Villas-Boas have attained the same success at another Portuguese club? Of course not. But would FC Porto have achieved the same with another coach? Of course not, either. Because that special combination is rare. As Mourinho and Villas-Boas have shown in recent times, both at the same place. In over 30 years of Porto's dominance, only these two coaches have managed to become greater than the club in terms of the feats they accomplished. The only point that should be of concern to a club, when they have one of these special beings, is to provide them with all the necessary conditions for them to create that impact. And to try and hold onto them for as long as possible. That part, however, is more difficult. Uncontrollable."

5

MR 15 MILLION

*"If I'd wanted to have an easy job, I would have stayed at
FC Porto – beautiful blue chair, the UEFA Champions
League trophy, God, and after God, me."*

José Mourinho

The life of a coach is not at all easy when you have to replace José
Mourinho at the helm of a football team. Luigi Del Neri (Italian),
Victor Fernandez (Spanish) and José Couceiro (Portuguese) can
attest to that: three coaches who, in a single season, sat on FC
Porto's post-Mourinho bench and none of whom were later missed
by the club's supporters. The Israeli, Avram Grant, who surprisingly
took the place of the Special One at Chelsea, merely guided the
team for what was left of the 2007-08 season. In July 2008, there
followed the Brazilian Scolari, armed with an enviable CV and an
incredibly strong personality, but who was sent packing by Roman
Abramovich at the end of only seven months. At Inter, it was the
turn of the Spaniard Rafa Benítez, who by November 2010 had
already received public ultimatums from President Massimo
Moratti because of the poor results that the Italian and European
champions were chalking up.

At around that time, André Villas-Boas was said to have been
the target for Inter. This led to a vehement denial by the manager at
the press conference which preceded the Portuguese Cup match
against Moreirense, as he labelled the news "absolutely ridiculous,
untimely and nonsensical. I was lucky enough to be at that club, I
know the people who head it and I know this news is nothing but
speculation. Apart from that, I intend to be here at Porto for a long

time," he confirmed. Benítez managed to stay on at Inter until December, but ended up being replaced by the Brazilian Leonardo, who also did not make it past the end of the 2010-11 season.

In fact, as the season came to an end, not even winning the Coppa Italia was of any real consolation. Leonardo began to be touted as the future Sporting Director at Paris Saint-Germain, as a consequence of the sale of 70% of the club's shares to Qatar Sports Investments, who were seeking to strengthen the club's structure. This provoked the president at Inter to comment "it's best that he follow his aspirations and that we look for a new coach," stating further that despite all of Leonardo's "goodwill and passion… it is obvious that being at Inter is not his aspiration for the future."

Moratti, with the help of Javier Zanetti, captain of both Inter and Argentina's national team, then contacted Marcelo Bielsa in order to head the team in the 2011-12 season. The Argentine coach, dubbed "El Loco" and who is known for presenting predominantly attacking football teams, had left the Chilean national team after a dispute with the recently elected president of the Chilean FA. However, he turned Inter Milan down as he had already made a commitment to Josu Urrutia, who was running for president at Athletic Bilbao (and who, in fact, went on to win the elections). All of this took place on 15 June, 2011.

Previously, however, at the end of May, the Italian press had already been talking about the possibility of an imminent meeting between Moratti and André Villas-Boas, to take place in Milan. "If Villas-Boas does come to Milan, I don't believe it is because of us. We already know him. We know that Villas-Boas has a lot of quality, but we are not going to change our coach (Leonardo)," explained the Inter president.

Bielsa's refusal caught Moratti off guard, and made him once again think of Villas-Boas, even though other names were also mentioned as possibilities, including England coach, Fabio Capello, Delio Rossi (the former Palermo coach) and the Serbian Sinisa

Mihajlovic, a former player and former assistant coach at the club, who according to Sky Sport 24, was refused permission to meet with Milan by his club, Fiorentina.

Inter's interest in the young Portuguese coach led to all sorts of speculation in the press, and on 18 June while some stated that Villas-Boas had supposedly flown to Milan upon the invitation of Inter's president, others gave contradictory reports saying that the directors Marco Branca and Piero Ausilio were headed to Portugal to try and secure Villas-Boas in Leonardo's post. Even though Villas-Boas was on holiday, and therefore free to travel wherever he pleased, his agent, Carlos Gonçalves, immediately denied the news, confirming firstly that the story did "not make sense" and secondly that the manager had not been in Milan.

The speculations came to an end on 19 June. Inter's sporting director, Marco Branca, denied that the FC Porto manager would be the next coach of the Nerazzurri. "I have to clarify this because, understandably, this all came up in the media," Branca said to the Italian Newspaper Association, ANSA. And bringing the subject to a close, he explained: "Villas-Boas's connection to FC Porto is well-known in the footballing world, but that is not all; there is also the fact that the payment required under his release clause is very high, which excludes him from being a candidate for coach at Inter."

Apparently, however, the main reason why Inter backed down was to do with the fact that Chelsea were already on the scene and arranging to sign the Porto manager, and Inter were fully aware that the English club were more than able to pay the payment required under the release clause.

ABRAMOVICH ONCE MORE

Strangely enough, or perhaps not, not a single observation was heard from Pinto da Costa throughout the entire process, which after all lasted a little over two days. Not at all what the supporters would expect from the Porto president, which would have been something along the lines of what he had stated over the last months, that is, an announcement – yet another one – about the complete synchronization between Villas-Boas and the club in terms of their continued collaboration for the forthcoming 2011-12 season. On the contrary, on that Sunday 19 June, Pinto da Costa merely clarified the obvious: "Villas-Boas has a contract and a 15 million Euro clause. If someone deposits 15 million in our account and he wants to go, there is nothing we can do, because it is something that is contractually specified. If that doesn't happen, he doesn't leave. We are not going to facilitate negotiations one bit. He will only leave if they pay 15 million and he wants to go."

Less than a month before, on 23 May, in an interview with RTP (Portuguese Television Channel) his response to the exact same question had been very different: "It's non-negotiable. Firstly, because he doesn't want to leave. If André Villas-Boas didn't share the same passion that I have for FC Porto, which led me to say that he is in his "dream seat", I am convinced that he could leave. He has a release clause of 15 million, which is not so significant for certain clubs. But I am sure that if they come here with that clause, he will not want to leave. That's the advantage of him being a *portista*." [29]

When he said that nothing could be done if a club were to pay the release clause and the manager wanted to leave, Pinto da Costa wasn't referring to the advances from Inter. He already knew of Villas-Boas's intentions to set off for Chelsea. He had been informed by André the previous day, on Saturday 18 June, of his intended departure to the British capital, though it had caught him by surprise.

The English press wrote that Abramovich had flown out to meet Villas-Boas that very Saturday, but that the FC Porto manager had

---

29. *Portista is the name for a supporter of FC Porto*

not given his immediate agreement. It was only the next day, on the Sunday, that he pledged his commitment to the directors at Chelsea.

Although Porto's supporters were completely unaware of what was happening "backstage", they were nonetheless used to the way the club's president usually spoke of these matters. And so, it was natural that they should interpret Pinto da Costa's announcement with the greatest apprehension. After all, they didn't want to see their manager leave, as he had brought them so much happiness and glory in a single season at the helm of FC Porto. But the way the president had spoken had left them feeling that all was not well.

From apprehension to being in a state of shock took all but a few hours. What they had least wanted to hear was the breaking news on the Monday morning, 20 June: "Villas-Boas to coach Chelsea", was the headline on practically every Portuguese media website. The news, which caught almost everybody by surprise, started out as a strong possibility, and ended up in a whirlwind of information, just waiting to become official – something that would only be confirmed when Villa-Boas, or Chelsea on his behalf, deposited the 15 million release clause amount in FC Porto's bank account.

The fans thought back to Pinto da Costa's words the night before, which had been much less incisive than usual, and their apprehension could not have been any greater. Furthermore, although the transfer had not yet been carried out, nobody doubted Abramovich's capacity to pay the amount required under the release clause. Although it was the highest ever in football history for a manager, for a Russian tycoon who was one of the wealthiest men in the world it was still a relatively modest amount and possibly even a bargain.

Porto supporters had already got used to having the West London club drawing their reinforcements from the Dragon Stadium and paying high prices to do so. From Ricardo Carvalho (30 million) to André Villas-Boas, passing through Paulo Ferreira (20 million), Bosingwa (20 million) and even Mourinho (6 million), the investment made by Abramovich in FC Porto's assets stands at over 90 million Euros.

On that Monday, 20 June, at the end of the morning, while a delegation from Chelsea was in Portugal taking care of all the details related to the signing of Villas-Boas, FC Porto, through its SAD[30], issued a statement formally saying that "upon request of the CMVM (Portuguese Securities Market Commission), we hereby inform the market that the coach André Villas-Boas, as well as various players on the squad, has a release clause. Up until the present date, this society has received no notification that this clause would be exercised, nor the agreement of the coach as to this desideratum."

But the agreement between André Villas-Boas and Chelsea was indeed finalised. FC Porto, in fact, never considered negotiating the release clause, although that possibility was entertained by Villas-Boas, whose behaviour in this particular case was completely different to that when, only a short time before, Roma had tried to win him over with a phenomenal contract.

In effect, at the start of the process, not even AVB believed that Chelsea would pay the 15 million Euros. By accepting the clause and not disputing it, the Russian millionaire's club were dependent on the coach's wishes, and those had already been expressed. Villas-Boas accepted the offer, left Porto and moved to Madrid for two days, though many thought that he was still at home. Journalists, misled by the presence of a group of security guards outside his house in Foz, waited for him to appear, but in vain. Villas-Boas was not at home, and would leave for London direct from Madrid.

On Tuesday, 21 June, once again in the late morning, a new statement from FC Porto SAD explained that it had that very day been "notified of the intention of its coach, André Villas-Boas, to

---

30. SAD - Sociedade Anónima Desportiva – Society of Soccer Sports.

terminate without just cause the employment contract in force with this sports society, immediately triggering the respective release clause. Accordingly, the employment contract will be considered, by this society, to be terminated upon the deposit of the amount foreseen therein." If anyone still had any doubts or hopes that the young manager might stay on at the Dragon, this definitely settled the matter. After only one season, the reign of André Villas-Boas at FC Porto had come to an end.

One day after FC Porto, it was the turn of the London club to confirm the signing of the coach whom the English were starting to call Mini-Mourinho: "Chelsea Football Club is delighted to announce that André Villas-Boas will be the club's new manager. He has signed a three-year contract and will start work immediately."

TRAITOR!

FC Porto's supporters were not happy; not only as a result of Villas-Boas's departure, but mainly because of how he had left: without giving the club any room for manoeuvre, presenting his departure as a *fait accompli*, with the new season just around the corner.

The main problem, and here those who are close to the manager say he failed, was that he continued to say that he was in his dream seat right up until a few days before leaving FC Porto. For many fans this was incomprehensible. Those who know him say he was not careful about this detail – perhaps it would have been enough for him to smile, as he had so often done, whenever he was asked if he was leaving FC Porto, especially at a time when news of his possible departure or, at least, of the big European clubs' interest in him, was spreading like wildfire around the world.

On 28 June in the sports paper, *A Bola*, Miguel Sousa Tavares, one of FC Porto's best-known supporters, wrote an article that captured the feelings of the members and fans of the champion Portuguese club: "I personally hope that Mr Abramovich and Chelsea never become European champions, because I like to think that money cannot buy everything. I therefore renew my wishes of total sporting unhappiness to André Villas-Boas, during his stay at the helm of Mr Abramovich's footballing toy. The man who, even up until a month ago, I and all the Porto supporters lavished thanks and praise on, not only deserted us at the first opportunity of being covered in gold, but will now dedicate himself to dismantling, from a distance and for his own benefit, the team he once led."

Miguel Sousa Tavares [31] was referring to the new investments that Chelsea, according to the Portuguese press, were believed to be preparing to make by buying various FC Porto players. The most likely possibilities were João Moutinho (release clause of 40m Euros), Falcao (30m) and Hulk (100m), some of the most important players from the Dragons' fantastic 2010-11 season.

On the other hand, journalist Bruno Prata [32], in an article published on 21 June in the newspaper *Público*, felt that although the victory in Dublin had catapulted the name of André Villas-Boas, "it had been reasonable for the Porto supporters to believe that the great grandson of the 1st Viscount of Guilhomil would not abdicate from his 'golden seat' just yet. Because of his proclaimed *portismo* (love of FC Porto), because of the 15 million euro clause and because of the guarantee that he would have an even stronger team at FC Porto in order to promote the image of the club (and his own) in the Champions League, which obviously is on a different scale to the Europa League. Multiplying his current salary by five and coaching one of the top three squads in the world, which Chelsea is,

---

31. *Miguel Sousa Tavares is one of the most highly respected Portuguese journalists, a television commentator, a best-selling author and one of the most influential opinion makers in Portugal. He is well-known for his portismo (love of FC Porto), which he expresses on a weekly basis in his column in the sports daily A Bola.*
32. *Bruno Prata is a journalist and commentator who is usually well informed on matters related to FC Porto.*

ended up persuading Villas-Boas to change his mind. It's human that he went back on his word, especially because this period in London allows him to stay on the course that led his former patron to success. And also because, in football, the train doesn't always stop twice at the same platform."

Bruno Prata's interpretation of the Villas-Boas's decision was confirmed by the manager himself. At Chelsea's presentation press conference he publicly stated that "all I could do was to take advantage of this opportunity and I did so against everyone's wishes, including those of my family, who were very reluctant. It was a difficult personal decision, but a lucid one."

The idea that he had basically gone after the money – as he would go from earning 1m per season at FC Porto to 5m at Chelsea – was purposely denied by Villas-Boas himself, when at the same conference he stated surprisingly: "I admit that there were commitments, through what I said, that increased the feeling of disloyalty among FC Porto's supporters. But what I said at the time was sincere. It was hard, very hard, the separation. The Portuguese journalists that are here are my witnesses, and they know the repercussions that my leaving FC Porto had. My commitment to Porto was 100%. But after an intensive year, crazy even, with lots of success and trophies, I felt I needed a new challenge. I needed to take a risk and challenge myself. In the end, Porto made a very good, very competitive counter-offer for me to stay on, but even so I preferred to leave, especially because once you have won everything you might make the mistake of becoming overly confident, and neglect details, leading you to make needless mistakes."

Luís Freitas Lobo summed it up best when he wrote incisively that "the market, as we knew it, changed in 2004 with the entry of stratospheric money coming from outside the up-until-then normal circuit. The appearance of Abramovich and the oligarchy that supports him, the origin of that new money, adulterated the normal functioning of the major deals and transfers. After him, came the Arab fortunes. Money outside what was naturally generated by the football industry broke into the industry and has become an invisible time bomb that may explode at any moment. In other words, before, with the big clubs and their normal boards, these moves took place more naturally; but now with these new tycoons, this is impossible to foresee. Everything can change at any given moment. Even the most sincere oaths of love. The unbearable lightness of football beings becomes exposed in a flash. After great international success, to think that the fragile financing of Portuguese football and its successful exponents (coaches and players) could remain impermeable or insensitive to all of this is to live outside of reality. It is a lost war."

"I have aspired to this position (of manager at FC Porto) in a crazy and blind manner. It's the position I want, the club where I grew up and which I support. It is the highest position I have aspired to. I've been able to achieve this goal at an early stage in my career, but I am fully aware that I am not here to play and that I have the competency to keep this team on the road to success. That is what I want to do. It is not up to me to say how long I'll be here. I hope to be successful and to rise to the occasion."

It was through remarks such as these, scattered here and there throughout his time at FC Porto (the one above dates from January 2011) that André Villas-Boas created a strong and emotional bond with the fans. And therefore, with his sudden departure he naturally became a traitor – and will remain so until the anger of the fans abates and their thanks for so many and such brilliant past victories once again places him in that spot that FC Porto's history will inevitably reserve for him. After all, the same thing has already happened with José Mourinho.

Those who did not consider André Villas-Boas to be a traitor in the least were the players he led at FC Porto. All those who voiced an opinion clearly showed their solidarity with the manager's decision to move to London. This was illustrated by the statements made by the captain, Helton, when he said that "everyone wishes the best for others. We will not forget him, just as he will not forget this group." And he continued to share what he was feeling, saying "we have to wish him the best. He chose what he thought was best for him and for the club. We have to thank him, even for being a friend." But he did not stop there. "I think that the whole of Portugal has a lot to thank André Villas-Boas for, because he has left behind many good things, as did José Mourinho," confirmed the captain. Central defender Rolando, another of the key members of the team throughout the 2010-11 season, said publicly that André Villas-Boas had his telephone number, and that all he had to do was call if he wanted him at Chelsea. What more can the leader of a group wish for when he leaves that group behind and continues to enjoy the admiration and friendship of those that worked with him?

"A ship in port is safe; but that's not what ships are built for." This quote, more than anything else, illustrates the decision that André Villas-Boas had to take. And the word port (porto in Portuguese) may be interpreted in two different ways: literally, as port, the safe harbour to which the author of the above sentence was referring; but also as Porto, the club which is a veritable guarantor of stability and success for a football professional. It just so happened that the ship *Villas-Boas* was ready to leave port and set off on other adventures on the high seas of European football.

THE GHOST OF MOURINHO

As far as the Porto president was concerned, however, the former manager of the Dragons had other reasons for leaving. A little over two weeks after André Villas-Boas's departure, Pinto da Costa gave a public interview to the journalist Fátima Campos Ferreira. He disclosed a conversation he'd had with Villas-Boas, after the manager had revealed he was afraid of losing the European Super Cup to Barcelona.

"Are you worried about shipping three or four goals against Barcelona?"

"If we do concede three or four and I do badly in the Champions League, nobody will want me next year."

"You're worried about three or four goals, but Mourinho conceded five goals against Barça and he was still the best in the world."

The Porto leader then went on to conclude: "So, it is obvious that he was afraid he couldn't replicate the success he'd enjoyed. The ghost of Mourinho is always there, and as Mourinho won the UEFA Cup and then the Champions League, he didn't want to risk a second season where he could be compared negatively to Mourinho for only having won one year and lost in the second. I think that was as important as the truck full of pounds that stopped outside his door."

Well humoured and totally at ease, he added that "if I were his father, I would have told him the same thing I said as a president and friend: that he should stay at Porto for one more year. In football, when you speak of the European giants, the gauge isn't Chelsea, it's Real Madrid, Barcelona or Manchester United."

Pinto da Costa feels that Villas-Boas would have had every possibility to progress in his career if he had spent one more season at the club. "I told him that this will probably be Guardiola's last season at Barcelona and that Barça is the best club for him, but he was afraid of being compared to Mourinho and left."

Thus, for the Porto president this was not about a personal challenge. It was only about a fear-provoking ghost on the one hand, and a pile of pounds on the other.

Asked to respond to Pinto da Costa's statements, André Villas-Boas merely repeated what he'd been saying since he had left the Dragon: "I know the president of FC Porto well and I respect him.

Everybody knows that FC Porto is my club. What we left there will always mean a great deal to me and to the club itself. But that's how it is; it was a difficult separation, as I have always said."

However, it seems obvious that if André Villas-Boas really was living with the ghost of Mourinho, then Chelsea would have been the very last club he would have chosen to leave FC Porto for. Precisely because at Stamford Bridge the comparisons with the Special One will be even more inevitable and the pressure of Mourinho's shadow is sure to follow him from the first to the last minute of his days in London. As he himself admitted on that same occasion: "If I had a Mourinho problem, I wouldn't have come to Chelsea for sure. Because he was extra successful in the years here, and it's a club that is looking for the Holy Grail (of winning the Champions League). So, if I'm escaping the Holy Grail of Porto, I'm running into trouble trying to find it in this club that has been fighting for it for a long time."

Nonetheless, the financial effort that FC Porto was willing to undertake in order to secure André Villas-Boas, and to which Pinto da Costa did not refer, came as a truly surprising revelation. Not because of the attitude in itself, but essentially because of the amount in question, as we know today how much Villas-Boas went to earn in London. Surprising, but it also confirms that Pinto da Costa was willing to do almost anything in order not to dismantle a team he believed would follow in the footsteps of the 2003 team, who after winning the UEFA Cup went on to win the Champions League in the following season. "Various stars were asked to stay for one more year, on the assumption that there would be a team (and a coach) with the necessary abilities to add to its value," wrote Bruno Prata in the previously mentioned article published in the daily paper *Público*.

RISKS, DOUBTS AND... REVOLUTIONS

The leader Villas-Boas had just left (Pinto da Costa) transmits as much stability to his managers as the one he was about to meet (Roman Abramovich) transmits instability. Although he has turned the club into one of the strongest in Europe, thanks to hefty investments underwritten by his personal fortune, in eight years the Russian tycoon has already had seven different coaches. Something generally less common in England, where coaches tend to enjoy rather more enduring working relationships with clubs and are not sacked at every turn as they are in Portugal.

Abramovich's latest victim was the Italian, Carlo Ancelotti, who has a CV that speaks for itself. He was summarily dismissed 12 months after giving Chelsea the first double in their history and, in his second season at the helm of the team, taking the club to second place in the Premier League, thus guaranteeing their direct access to the Champions League group phase. He was informed of his dismissal by the club's executive director, Ron Gourlay, even before leaving Goodison Park, Everton's stadium, where Chelsea had played on the last day of the 2010-11 season.

But André Villas-Boas is well aware of what he is getting himself into. "What you expect from this club is to be successful straight away," he stated at the presentation press conference at Chelsea. And he himself concluded that "I'd be surprised to be kept on if I don't win." During his time as manager of Chelsea, José Mourinho had spoken about this in a similar vein in a reference he made to Rafa Benitez, Liverpool's coach at the time: "Three years without any titles? I'd be unemployed."

In England, many people have expressed doubts about Abramovich's new gamble – mostly because of Villas-Boas's age, he is the youngest ever manager to work in the Premier League; but also because he passed by largely unnoticed at Chelsea when he worked there as a member of José Mourinho's technical staff. In fact, the club's employees remember Villas-Boas as a very quiet person, who lived in the shadow of the Special One, and spent a great deal of time away observing matches. On his return he would then shut himself away in his office producing the reports. All the players liked André, he could even be called a popular figure at the club and nobody ever had anything negative to say about him – but, truth be told, he was always in that shadow.

Pedro Pinto, a Portuguese journalist who works for CNN in London, even wrote that he had lost count of how many people had asked him how to pronounce the name of the man who was ever so close to becoming Chelsea's new manager. And Paul Scholes, who had just hung up his boots and joined Alex Fergusson's staff at Manchester United, admitted that he had not heard of André Villas-Boas before that June – that is the very moment that he was confirmed as the Chelsea manager! Scholes also took the opportunity to add, diplomatically, that "he comes across as someone who knows exactly what he wants and he has had a good grounding with (José) Mourinho and Bobby Robson."

Graeme Souness, a leading figure in the midfield of the mighty Liverpool team that dominated European football in the late 1970s and early 1980s, was one of the first to raise questions over the choice of the young Portuguese coach. Souness worked in Portugal between 1997 and 1999 as Benfica's manager, and that fact perhaps gave him the legitimacy to state in an interview with Sky Sports that Villas-Boas "had a great year last season, but he's a novice and I think it's an enormous gamble. It's not the hardest job in the world to win the league with Porto. Because of the way things are structured at the club, starting with the president, their success is more or less guaranteed every year." And the Scotsman knew what he was talking about, as he himself had lost the Portuguese championship to FC Porto. But Souness's reasoning went a little further: "Having won the Europa League with Porto, he deserves a lot of credit for that, but the Europa League is not a priority." In relation to his age, he had this advice to give: "What he's got to do immediately is get the players on his side. At 33, some of them will be older than him and he's a novice any way you look at it."

At 26 years of age, Berger, one of André Villas-Boas's players at Académica, had the following to say about the manager being so young: "There was never any confrontation between him and the older players. He always tried to help the players and told us that if we ever had any problems to go and talk to him. This was very important – everyone could speak to him." And, showing great faith in André Villas-Boas's future at the London club, he said: "He places a lot of importance on creating a great team spirit, so everyone works together and roots for the group. He has a great personality and we as players can feel it. We want to work with him and do everything well for him."

Even though he was rarely selected by Villas-Boas at FC Porto, the Brazilian midfielder Souza, had something similar to say when questioned about their manager – a manager who not only looked like a player, but was young enough to be one: "I don't find it strange. He imposes respect, and speaks very well with all the players." This view was also shared by the team captain Helton, the oldest player on the squad, when he stated that "many might view his age as a problem. I don't. Very often one's age doesn't match one's mind. There are older people who often do not manage to be respected by those who are younger. As for qualities – and by this I do not mean that older people aren't the same – I must emphasise the way he is always "in sync" with the players, as well as the way he manages to transmit his ideas more quickly." Thus, for Helton, the issue of age was not seen as a disadvantage, but rather it worked to his advantage.

For his part, André Villas-Boas did not avoid the issue, and in response to a question by the *Sunday Mirror* he explained: "I accept people may view it as a gamble employing someone so young, but if I didn't believe I could succeed, what is the point?" And at the presentation as the new Chelsea manager he once again addressed the issue by acknowledging that "it's normal for people to judge me by my age. Everything happened to me early, from the age of 18 up to now, naturally, over time. The players are professional and responsible; I've never had a problem with anyone."

In a question raised by a Russian journalist, before FC Porto's match against Spartak Moscow for the Europa League, he was asked how the players treated him. He explained: "They call me Boss, naturally, with the utmost respect. In this working group, everyone knows their place, there are absolutely no problems. Lack of respect? There's no room for that. The manager decides, for better or for worse, and the players know that's the way it goes. Being young has no effect."

At the end of Chelsea's Asian tour, while referring to the team spirit he had managed to implement at FC Porto, he commented that "the (Chelsea) players were able to assimilate that spirit. To sell ideas the players have to buy them, and this is happening."

And in one of the rare exclusive interviews he granted, in *Diário de Coimbra* at the end of the 2009-10 season, when he was managing Académica, Villas-Boas explained very clearly how he views the question of leadership: "Players always measure up their leader and are always looking for his weaknesses and testing those weaknesses. On the other hand, when they are faced with competency, rigour and organisation they don't look for those weak points, but rather they strive to make those first three qualities evident." Without having the opportunity to read this interview, Gary Lineker had something similar to say when he stated that "the Chelsea players will know pretty quickly if André Villas-Boas has something special or not. If he has, he'll be fine; if he hasn't, he will soon be found out. And the murmurings from the dressing room will begin. He's going to need a really big personality."

Spurs manager, Harry Redknapp, simplified the issue and

presented a different view: "It's a great job. You would have to be a fool not to do a good job at Chelsea, with those players. You walk into the dressing room and look around and see great players, leaders like John Terry, Frank Lampard, and Didier Drogba. It would be hard to fail."

In other words, only someone incompetent – which André Villas-Boas has already shown he isn't – can fail at Chelsea. Where, then, lay the risk everybody was talking about? Perhaps in the volatility of the club's owner.

Suddenly it seemed that everyone was qualified to give an opinion on the new Chelsea boss. Olivier Dacourt, who in England has played for Everton, Leeds and Fulham, is not exactly an opinion maker, and at age 36, he is no longer playing at the highest level. What interest, therefore, could there be in hearing what he had to say about André Villas-Boas? In fact, the former French international worked at Inter for a year with Mourinho, where he had the opportunity to get to know the young André. He could not be more complimentary about him and told BBC Sport that "we have seen the student outgrow the teacher in the past and this could happen now with Villas-Boas at Chelsea. He learnt much from Mourinho but he is very different. He is more human." He admitted that he had had problems with Mourinho, but that Villas-Boas had acted as if nothing had happened – not what usually happens when a player has a problem with the manager and it affects relationships with the whole coaching staff. "As well as being a top coach, he's a fantastic person. And the players all loved him," he revealed.

Comparing the FC Porto squad that AVB worked with in the 2010-11 season with the squad he will find at Chelsea, Gary Lineker explained his point of view: "It's all very well at Porto, where you have decent players but not big household names. It's going to be hard to go into a dressing room with players who have been at the club for many years."

And so, many expected that Villas-Boas would make great

changes to the squad, precisely to avoid the problem raised by Lineker. People even began mentioning the name of Frank Lampard, team vice-captain, and one of the club's historic and most charismatic players. But the manager, who at FC Porto calmly accepted working with all the players who were a part of the squad, immediately made it clear that he would not go down that road: "When a new manager appears, everybody immediately thinks about revolutions, but with a club that's been successful for six or seven years, adjustments must be carefully made and thoughtful decisions taken."

This explanation, however, did not bring the matter to a close. In Kuala Lumpur, Malaysia, the first of Chelsea's many stops on their Asian pre-season tour, André Villas-Boas felt it necessary to return to this subject, especially since there continued to be much speculation in the media about a possible "clean-up" in the dressing room. Once again, he went over the ideas he had put forward from the moment he had signed with Chelsea, but this time he referred to three of the most important players on the squad and asked reporters some questions of his own: "The untouchables? Untouchable is a person who continuously performs at a high level. Based on the trophies these players have won before and the success they have had, aren't these the players you want in the end? Could be, no?" And he continued with an explanation that essentially served to clarify many of the doubts raised as to his capacity to lead players, such as the three referred to. "The most important thing for a leader is to be coherent in the decisions he takes and it's a principle I cannot let go of. As long as their performance allows them to fight for a place in the starting eleven, they deserve opportunities."

SCOLARI AND THE CHELSEA DRESSING ROOM

Although the leadership principles set out by Villas-Boas are clear and from the outset, just, fears regarding the possible difficulties that he might encounter managing the dressing room at Chelsea lead us to recall the experience of the former Portugal national coach, Luiz Felipe Scolari [33], despite the fact that the two men have little in common.

When he arrived in London in July 2008, the Brazilian knew he was walking into a minefield – as he himself admitted to those closest to him, but never publicly. Everything began with the process of his signing. Chelsea's owner, Roman Abramovich, had chosen the Italian Carlo Ancelotti, but could not convince him to leave AC Milan. In favour of Scolari was Peter Kenyon, the club's managing director at the time, who was backed by Eugene Tenenbaum, one of Abramovich's trusted men and responsible for Chelsea's financial side. One week before the start of Euro 2008, Kenyon and Tenenbaum finally got the go ahead from Abramovich, and they worked everything out with Scolari, at his home in Cascais, Portugal.

On 1 June 2008, the day the Portuguese national side left for Switzerland, the Brazilian coach made a verbal agreement with Chelsea and informed Gilberto Madaíl, president of the Portuguese Football Federation about it. But what nobody was expecting was Abramovich's first demonstration of "I call the shots here". On the evening of 11 June, shortly after the end of the match between

---

33. *Luiz Felipe Scolari arrived at Chelsea (at the age of 59) with an enviable CV. Apart from various victories at club level in Brazil, his career had included two Liberators Cups (for Grémio de Porto Alegre in 1995 and Palmeiras in 1999), the World Cup in 2002 for Brazil, in the Korea-Japan World Cup, and the best ranking in the history of the Portuguese national side who made it to the Euro 2004 Final, where they lost to Greece. He is especially well-known for being able to form a true family in the working groups he leads, and for turning that group spirit into a decisive weapon to generate positive results.*

Portugal and the Czech Republic, Chelsea put the news of the signing of the Brazilian coach up on their website. This caused an enormous upset for Scolari and the entire Portuguese delegation. The timing could not have been more precise, as it happened just after the post-match conference.

That very morning, director Carlos Godinho had questioned the coach about the matter, and the Brazilian had guaranteed that although he had entered into the agreement with Chelsea, it would only be made public after the European Cup had come to an end. As soon as they found out what was happening, both men immediately tried to contact Gilberto Madaíl to tell him of the events. There followed long minutes of distress for the two, as Madaíl was already at Geneva airport, getting ready to return to Lisbon and had switched off his mobile phone. Finally, in the departure lounge, his secretary managed to contact him. He immediately left the airport and headed for the Neuchâtel hotel where the Portuguese national side were staying. Before appearing side by side, in front of the players, almost at the end of dinner, Madaíl and Scolari gathered for some time, as the Brazilian coach apologised for Chelsea's actions, which could not be controlled or avoided. The situation was not easy for either of the men, but they decided to face the Portuguese players with a smile on their face, trying to keep things calm.

This first shock made Scolari more certain of the suspicions he had had about the work that awaited him at Chelsea, especially with regard to the support he could expect from Abramovich. Forewarned, the Brazilian coach gave express orders to his agent, Jorge Mendes, and the respective lawyers, to be uncompromising in the defence of their interests in the drawing up of the contract that would bind both parties. The truth is that for almost three weeks (the first few days at Cobham and during the tour of China and Russia), Scolari worked for Chelsea without having signed a contract. But when he finally did sign, it was already with the guarantee that his expected dismissal before the end of the contract would be safeguarded in financial terms.

Scolari was at Chelsea a little less than eight months, and during that time it is said that he met with Abramovich on only three occasions. The first time, for five minutes, on the eve of his presentation to the press; the second, at a social function just before Christmas 2008. The last time was on the day after his dismissal. Strangely enough, it was on this last occasion that they spoke at most length and most seriously about the club.

"Perhaps if that conversation had taken place on the first day, and not on the last, he wouldn't have been dismissed," confessed one of Scolari's closest collaborators. And the Brazilian drew a rather grim picture of what was happening behind the scenes at Chelsea, especially of the power plays and splits within the team. Scolari could not have been any clearer: "Until you take the power away from the Francophones, you will never have a united group, with everybody fighting for the same objective," he told Roman Abramovitch in that farewell conversation.

Although the captain was John Terry, and one of the key figures was Frank Lampard, another Englishman, according to Scolari it was not the English who ruled the dressing room. The real leader, for better or for worse, was Ivory Coast player, Didier Drogba, who led the group of Francophone players that included his rival, Nikolas Anelka. For one reason or another, the cold war between Scolari and Drogba began when the coach picked Anelka as his first choice player. Accustomed to his status being undisputed, Drogba confronted the coach in a manner he did not appreciate and things began to turn sour.

In late November, Chelsea began to accumulate poor results – after an impressive series of consecutive wins at the start of the season – and the atmosphere amongst the team got worse. Apart from Drogba, Florent Malouda and Salomon Kalou also posed internal disciplinary problems for Scolari, as the Francophone group ostensibly marked their position, to the point that they freely violated the internal rule that everyone was to speak English during training. This caused other problems, this time among the group formed by various Portuguese and Brazilian players, who felt discriminated against by the Francophones.

Apart from Drogba's envy of Anelka (the only Francophone with whom Scolari was able to maintain a non-confrontational relationship), two other players were also important during the Brazilian's not altogether successful time at Chelsea – the German Michael Ballack and Ghana's Michael Essien.

The problem with Ballack related to the German's poor form (also affected by injuries) and Deco's arrival at the London club, where he competed against him for a place on the team. Scolari had expressly requested Deco, whilst Ballack considered himself to be an untouchable star, so much so that he directly challenged the opinions of the Brazilian coach on more than one occasion. It has been said that Ballack did not have many friends in the dressing room, but that that did not stop him from calling for differential treatment which, for most of the time, was not justified in the eyes of the coach or his team mates. It is true that, as a result of under par performances, Deco himself didn't at times justify the investment made in him, and that this also added to the controversy, as it was felt that he was being selected only because of his closeness to the coach.

The relationship with Essien was completely different. Although he spoke French, having spent much of his career in French clubs, Essien did not fit in the group led by Drogba and Malouda. Due to an injury, he didn't play for almost the entire time Scolari was at Chelsea, and the coach was in no doubt that this was one of the reasons for the team's weak performance during the most demanding period, around Christmas and New Year.

"Essien was one of the most committed and dedicated professionals I have ever worked with. Above all, there are few men like him in football," the Brazilian said, some months after being dismissed from Chelsea, in a conversation among friends. Scolari also recalled that the Ghana midfielder didn't use his injury as an excuse to distance himself from the group. "He could have just stayed at the gym or with the physiotherapists, but he always came by the pitch and the dressing room, encouraging his team mates and wagging his finger at those he thought weren't giving their all to the team."

The tension between the Brazilian coach and part of the squad began to increase as from November 2008, with Scolari feeling that he was not getting any formal support from Chelsea's management.

"I knew I hadn't been Abramovich's first choice and that I ran the risk of not making it to the end of the first year, but I couldn't pass up the challenge of managing Chelsea," he later confessed to those closest to him. And the Brazilian rejects the argument that it was his limited English that brought about the failure. "In a group that is so linguistically diversified, what failed was not that, but rather that I wasn't able to impose my system of 'family' within the team. It's been that 'family' spirit that has always helped me everywhere, except at Chelsea, especially because a significant part of the group was against this and boycotted my attempt to build a family spirit," Scolari added in that meeting with friends who had closely followed his journey.

Today, it is with great interest that Scolari keeps up with the arrival of André Villas-Boas at a place that once was his. The Brazilian believes that Villas-Boas has various advantages in relation to himself, starting with the fact that AVB already knows Chelsea well and is not walking into Cobham as an unknown. Having worked with José Mourinho will not have been the most important aspect in Abramovich's choice, according to Scolari. More important, is the fact that he was precisely the Russian's personal choice, against various opinions from the club directors. It is said that Abramovich places a great deal of importance on the chronological coincidence of Mourinho's success at FC Porto and then at Chelsea, firmly believing that the same will happen with Villas-Boas. And as is now the case with Villas-Boas, in 2004 Mourinho was also not the choice of his advisors on the Board of the West London club.

Thus, Scolari feels that Villas-Boas will not have to face the problems he experienced in 2008, and that when he feels the need to "clean up" the dressing room, he will be able to count on the unconditional support of Chelsea's owner. "They're in for a difficult time if they think they can play around with André just because of his boyish face," he said from São Paulo, when asked about the young Portuguese manager's challenge. "André is good and he'll prove it again at Chelsea," he emphasised.

SECOND CHOICE?

Interestingly, just like Luiz Felipe Scolari, who was a second choice after a failed attempt to sign Ancelotti, André Villas-Boas too, according to the British press, was signed after Dutchman Guus Hiddink took too long to decide whether to take the post. "Chelsea turned to Villas-Boas due to Hiddink's reluctance to take on an all-encompassing role, which seems to have cost him his return to Stamford Bridge in the short term," wrote *The Times*. The paper also reported that Hiddink, who until recently was coach of Turkey, had been offered the position of Chelsea manager "last month, but that he had reservations and Chelsea grew wary of his evasions."

The *Daily Mail*, went further and explained that Hiddink was, at first, keen on moving to London, but then demanded "a top coach working alongside him to shoulder the burden." The paper went on to say that after being turned down by other coaches – Dutch Marco van Basten and the British Steve Clarke – the Blues turned to Villas-Boas, but "it soon became clear he would only consider the job of manager" and never that of assistant coach. *The Independent* confirmed this version: "The club had originally turned to Villas-Boas as a coach to work under Hiddink, but were so impressed by the Porto manager that they had decided to offer him the manager's job."

Chelsea's most important players knew André Villas-Boas from his time as part of José Mourinho technical staff. Nevertheless, it was commented that footballers like Drogba or Lampard, only a few months younger than André Villas-Boas, may have questioned the choice of the young manager, especially because of his lack of experience as a manager abroad. On the other hand, it was also said that Villas-Boas had been immediately accepted, largely as a result of John Terry's influence. Apparently, the name of André Villas-Boas had been mentioned to the Chelsea captain and he did not hesitate to give his approval. In fact, it is well known that Terry and Villas-Boas enjoyed a close relationship when they worked together at the club between 2004 and 2007.

"Terry is the captain and he'll be so for many years. He represents the club's history of success in the last six seasons; he is a point of reference," stated Villas-Boas at his first opportunity as the new Chelsea boss.

"Appointing Villas-Boas was not a brave decision, but a very good decision. We have spoken about managers coming and going, but I'm certain he will be around for a long time," said Terry in return, the first time he spoke in public after André's appointment. And he recalled Villas-Boas's previous spell at the club: "He was the guy that travelled the world looking for players, and we were very impressed with his knowledge even then. What he has achieved away from Chelsea has been incredible. Not enough chances are given to young managers... thankfully our owner has given him an opportunity." And he complimented him on his working methods, saying, "He knows what he wants from each player and he is very intelligent."

Some of the dressing room heavyweights had, in the meantime, also come out in defence of Roman Abramovich's new gamble. Petr Cech, who arrived at the club with José Mourinho in 2004, and has been at Stamford Bridge for a full seven seasons, was one of the first voices to be heard. In interviews in *The Sun* and on *BBC Radio 5*, he stated: "I haven't spoken to the manager yet, but I know him from the time he was here with Mourinho. André did a fantastic job then with all his analyses of our opponents, which I always found a big, big help. His knowledge of English football and Chelsea will also make a difference now."

According to the Chelsea goalkeeper, the tender age of the new manager cannot be seen as a problem. "He's already proven that he can lead a big club to success. He won the Europa League with FC Porto, which shows quality. If you are 16 and have the qualities to play at the highest level, then that's fine. It's the same for a young manager." The Czech international has known seven different managers since arriving at the club, and is hopeful that Villas-Boas will be around for a long time. "Now we have a young manager who can hopefully stay for 25 years like Ferguson at Manchester United. It would be great to have that continuity here!"

In comments to Chelsea's website, left-back Ashley Cole was also convinced that the manager wouldn't have any problems dealing with the squad. "Age is just a number; he has experience of being at Porto, a big club. Hopefully he can bring that glory to Chelsea, but I don't think the age thing is anything to worry about, I don't think the players think about that. He is our manager now and we have to go out and fight for him." And he went on to explain: "Whatever manager comes in we respect him, we are not kids. Everyone thinks there are egos at Chelsea, but there aren't." As for the work Villas-Boas had carried out at Chelsea previously, Cole was very clear: "The detailed way in which he explained the strengths and weaknesses of the opponents was impressive. He would inform Mourinho about all the players we would face."

FROM COACH TO MANAGER

Another of the doubts raised about Villas-Boas's appointment at Chelsea related to the functions he had carried out at FC Porto and those that would become a part of his job description in London.

At FC Porto the functions of a manager are essentially related only to coaching. There, Villas-Boas found a structure that was already completely established and flexible enough to respond to the smallest thing: a structure that he already knew from his time at Porto as part of Mourinho's technical staff; and a structure that many credit with playing a key role in the high rate of success that coaches who arrive at FC Porto seem invariably to enjoy.

At the head of that structure stands Pinto da Costa, president of both the club and SAD (Society of Soccer Sports), and Antero Henrique, general director of SAD; and it is they who set the guidelines. The coaches are responsible for maintaining the team's champion status – through the most appropriate tactical options – and ensuring strong leadership of the team.

In England, managers have much broader functions – hence the term. And if we take a close look at the commitment undertaken by Roman Abramovich in André Villas-Boas's first days of work at Chelsea, we will better understand the scale and scope of the responsibilities the young Portuguese was to assume at the London club. Scolari complained that he only spoke to the Russian tycoon on three occasions. The last of which was apparently the most productive, and took place only after he had already been sacked. André Villas-Boas, however, has been seen a number of times with Abramovich – both dressed casually, in jeans and a light shirt – accompanied by security guards, and going into one of the four-star hotels the club owns near Stamford Bridge. There, they have met in a VIP room exclusively reserved for executives, far from the prying eyes of the hotel's guests, in a type of meeting that the hotel employees themselves say is most unusual for the Russian boss.

After his appointment, there followed some frenetic working days – his first, on Wednesday 22 June, started at 9.30 am and only finished late evening – preparing for Chelsea's imminent future, with his family in Portugal allowing him to concentrate exclusively on the many things that needed doing at the club.

And André Villas-Boas's decisions immediately became known; such as the cancellation of the first pre-season game against Vitesse Arnhem in Holland, or the dismissals of Paul Clement (Assistant First-team Coach, 8 years with the club), Glen Driscoll (Fitness Coach) and Dr. Bryan English (Medical Director).

The last issue of *The News of the World*, closed down following the phone-hacking scandal, revealed a set of rules imposed by André Villas-Boas that would radically alter discipline within the club. With the aim of avoiding the problems of the recent past and building a united team from the outset, he took a series of measures that, even to the most suspicious, immediately began to demonstrate the strong personality of the youngest-ever manager in the Premier League.

Throughout this book, we have already seen how important the human factor is to André Villas-Boas, and the way in which he masters the difficult art of managing and motivating groups. Mourinho is perhaps the greatest master of this art, and André Villas-Boas is certain to have learnt a great deal from him. When Mourinho arrived at Chelsea, he asked the players who among them had won any titles, knowing full well that apart from Ricardo Carvalho and Paulo Ferreira, players that had come with him from Porto to London, nobody else could boast of such a feat. Mourinho had also been looked upon with some suspicion because of his relative youth and because, at the highest level, he had managed only FC Porto. In this way, Mourinho clearly establised his position relative to the group with whom he was to work.

André Villas-Boas, on the other hand, walking into the same dressing room seven years later, found a group of players who had won various titles in the service of the club. According to *The News of the World*, he had all memorabilia of recent past glories removed from the Cobham training ground, including photographs of celebrations from the Mourinho or Ancelotti era. With this decision, he wanted the players to internalise the idea that with him everything would be starting anew, and as such the team had not yet won anything.

But the measures revealed by the now-defunct tabloid do not stop here. For instance, irrespective of the training hours, during the pre-season work, the players were always to be at Cobham for 9:00am and meals were to be taken in a group.

In addition, in order to avoid the formation of the mini-groups that Scolari referred to, he re-instituted English as the sole official language in the dressing room. Not at all surprising for those who know that things were exactly the same at FC Porto: the only language allowed was Portuguese. A mission made easier there by the fact that the squad were practically bilingual, speaking both Portuguese and Castilian.

As far as the treatment of injuries was concerned, players were forbidden from watching television, speaking on the telephone or reading the papers during treatments, so that these could be viewed more seriously. This was contrary to what had happened in previous years. Another objective was to turn the training ground into an exclusively professional area, and so players were forbidden from taking their friends, family, advisors, hairdressers and even their agents there.

For a young manager, about whom so many doubts had been raised, he quickly showed that those fears were unfounded as soon he started work. He did have the strength of character to impose himself on a team composed of players who were only just a little younger than him.

"They're in for a difficult time if they think they can play around with André just because of his boyish face," Scolari had warned.

6

MIRROR, MIRROR
ON THE WALL...

"Clearly he's learnt from José and there are certain things
where you think that is very Mourinho-esque."

John Terry

Does it make sense to say that Neymar is the new Pelé? Or that Messi is better than Maradona? Is it legitimate to compare the 1970s Brazil team to Guardiola's Barcelona? Probably not. In the same way, it doesn't make sense to repeat the now worn-out idea that Villas-Boas is the new Mourinho. Nevertheless, it is irresistible to compare the Special One and the Special Too (as we decided to call him in the title of this book), as a result of their past and the path they both share. Let's look at some of these points:

- They are both Portuguese.

- They were born with a strong passion for football.

- They were both unsuccessful footballers.

- Bobby Robson "gave them a hand" and allowed them to get a start in football at the highest level.

- They worked as (opponent) scouts on coaching staffs.

- They drew people's attention as coaches at modest clubs.

- They arrived at FC Porto before completing a full year in their career as head coaches.

- They stormed to success in their first season at FC Porto.

- They left FC Porto unexpectedly, against the wishes of the club, and went to work at Chelsea.

- They arrived at the Premier League without any other experience apart from the Portuguese League.

It seems, therefore, that there are probably more points that unite them than separate them. The opinions of those that have shared experiences with both, or of similarly placed specialists elsewhere, confirm that there are clearly similarities, in both form and content, between the two Portuguese coaches.

Let's start then with something that is purely objective: cold, hard numbers. The only logical comparison lies in their respective first complete seasons (in Villas-Boas's case, the only one) at FC Porto: the same club, the same structure, the same championship, the same cup and the same European competition (the UEFA Cup/ Europa League).

Both achieved a treble (Portuguese Championship, Portuguese Cup and UEFA/Europa League Cup). Villas-Boas managed to add the Portuguese Super Cup to that, a competition that Mourinho was not given the opportunity of playing in. However it is also true that Villas-Boas failed to win the League Cup, a trophy that didn't exist at the time of the Special One. And so, Mourinho won three out of three competitions, and Villas-Boas won four out of five.

Up until recently it was believed that José Mourinho had established unbeatable records in the history of FC Porto in the 2002-03 season. But the numbers do not confirm this. As we will see in a more detailed manner in the table we have set out on the next page, Mourinho had an efficiency rate of 77.3% in 53 matches at the helm of the team. Clearly lower than the 84.4% achieved by André Villas-Boas in the 2010-11 season. AVB was also involved in more matches (58) than Mourinho.

Looking at the defensive records, the figures are practically the same – Mourinho's FC Porto conceded an average of 0.74 goals per match, whilst the figure for Villas-Boas's FC Porto stands at 0.72. However, when you look at the attacking records, the "student" outdoes the "teacher" – Mourinho achieved an average of 2.23 goals per match, whilst Villas-Boas managed an impressive 2.50, confirming the commonly held observation that, at FC Porto, he implemented a system of play that favoured attacking football.

Let's take a look at the tables for each manager.

JOSÉ MOURINHO: FC Porto 2002-03

	G	W	D	L	Goals	Efficiency
League	34	27	5	2	73-26	79.4
Cup	6	6	0	0	16-3	100.0
UEFA Cup	13	8	2	3	29-10	61.5
Total	**53**	**41**	**7**	**5**	**118-39**	**77.3**

ANDRÉ VILLAS-BOAS: FC Porto 2010-11

	G	W	D	L	Goals	Efficiency
League	30	27	3	0	73-16	90.0
Cup	7	6	0	1	20-6	85.7
League Cup	3	1	1	1	6-4	33.3
Port. Sup. Cup	1	1	0	0	2-0	100.0
Europa L'gue	17	14	1	2	44-16	82.3
Total	**58**	**49**	**5**	**4**	**145-42**	**84.4**

Despite all the similarities we have described – club, structure, championship, cup, European competition – as the purists will say the situations and circumstances are never the same. This is true.

And in this particular case, the pendulum swings back in favour of Mourinho: he took over a directionless, broken team that had yet to taste success (they had won no titles under the previous manager Octávio Machado); whilst André Villas-Boas inherited a solid, organised group who were used to winning in their very recent past (three national championships, three Portuguese Cups and a Super Cup, in four years with Jesualdo Ferreira at the helm).

It would make absolutely no sense to carry out further comparisons, especially when looking at both careers overall. José Mourinho boasts 11 years as a manager, an unparalleled CV and armfuls of trophies that make him the best coach in the world; André Villas-Boas has just begun his third season (his second full one), with some very promising signs, it's true, but he is still leagues away from the numbers chalked up by the master. After all, as Villas-Boas himself admitted when Mourinho was considered the best in the world by FIFA in January 2011: "The uniqueness and exclusivity of the prize reveal what the career of José Mourinho is. With him, there are no limits. Everything that he sets out as an objective is immediately achieved. He has had a singular career, that has no comparison in history and will not have in the future." And he went on to add that "José Mourinho will become the best coach of all time, without a shadow of a doubt."

WITH THEIR NOSES IN THE AIR

André Villas-Boas is 14 years younger than José Mourinho. A big difference, perhaps in favour of the younger man as it offers, purely theoretically, the possibility of achieving even more success. Apart from being younger, Villas-Boas struck out on his own earlier: he was 31 years old when he became a head coach, while the current Real Madrid manager only stopped working under Louis van Gaal at the age of 37.

In terms of education, Villas-Boas only completed 12th grade, and then did coaching courses for the various levels established by UEFA. Mourinho, on the other hand, followed an academic path: he took a course in Sports in Lisbon, at the former Higher Institute for Physical Education, now known as the Faculty for Human Motricity.

The subject of "comparisons" bothers Mourinho and Villas-Boas alike, and both of them have indicated this on more than one occasion. The first public show of discomfort was on 3 June 2010, when André Villas-Boas was presented as the new manager at FC Porto. "I am not a clone of anybody, but if you want to talk about this, I think I am more a clone of Robson than of Mourinho. I have English ancestry, a big nose and I like drinking wine..."

The words echoed around the VIP room at the Dragon Stadium and eventually made their way to Madrid. Mourinho took two months and two days to retort, and did so scathingly in an interview with the Portuguese sports paper *Record*: "Don't compare him to me, because when I went to FC Porto I had already worked out on the pitch, which is quite different." Hostilities commenced and the reasons for such an abrupt "break up" were suddenly clear: you cannot have two roosters in the same coop. Less than a year after the above-mentioned exchange, Villas-Boas confirmed what everybody already considered as inevitable: "I don't speak to Mourinho."

André Villas-Boas's 'big nose', as he himself described it – and his avowed love of the red wines of the Alentejo and Douro regions – stands in stark contrast to José Mourinho's regular one, the nose of someone who only likes water and Coca-Cola. But this is merely an outward manifestation of the differences between them. They both sport the same 3-day stubble, but when it comes to hair it's a different matter. André's curly, ginger hair doesn't allow for many changes, in either hairstyle or in length, while Mourinho's greying hair has changed according to fashion: full of volume and gel-laden during his time as an assistant coach (in the 1990s) to today's more classic and natural look. Although the Real Madrid manager confessed in a 2006 interview to the weekly *Expresso* that it wasn't done purposely: "I go to my wife's hairdresser. He's a cool bloke. When she goes, I pick her up and he sets aside a few minutes for me and touches it up. But I don't pay any attention to it. In the summer, I shaved it off. Some people told me 'It's awful', while others said 'It looks great.' It's all the same to me. Now, I'm going to let it grow and then we'll see."

In terms of clothing, there are no significant differences. They both wear grey or black fitted suits, with a modern cut. José Mourinho is much more selective when it comes to designer labels. Villas-Boas does not wear a tie as often – not even on special occasions, such as his public presentations as manager at FC Porto or Chelsea. When he does wear one, however, he copies the master with a large reinforced knot and his top button undone. One thing is clear though: Mourinho is more style and image conscious than Villas-Boas. Perhaps this is where Villas-Boas begins to distance himself from the one-man-show style. "I think it's important for people not to focus on me. We have to open things up a bit – we have great players here and we've been in great European competitions, we've won English titles, and so that success that Chelsea is used to needs to be respected. This is not a one-man-show; rather it's the work of a whole group. You cannot credit it to one person, especially because I want to involve everybody in this project," the Chelsea manager said on the day of his presentation.

As for similarities in their gestures, the most interchangeable is probably one which relates to coats of all things. In April 2006, after the match that clinched the Premier League title from Manchester United – Mourinho's second title at Chelsea – the Portuguese manager did something rather unexpected. It was in the euphoria following the 3-0 win, when all Chelsea had needed was a draw. After the medals had been handed out the manager walked towards the Chelsea supporters who were sitting in the stand behind one of the goals. Once there, he tossed his medal into the stand, then took off his coat and also threw that to the fans – a symbolic homage to all those who were chanting his name. Some four years later, in Matosinhos, André Villas-Boas did the very same thing. In the third from last match of the Portuguese League, and after a hard-won and decisive 3-1 away victory against Leixões (a match that saved Académica from relegation), André walked towards the Mancha Negra, where Académica's supporters were, took off his coat and threw it into the stands. In an interview that he later gave to the newspaper *Diário de Coimbra* he was questioned about the similarity between his and Mourinho's act. Somewhat annoyed, the coach explained: "You're thinking in exactly the same way as those who search for ways to compare us. You're not looking at the spontaneity, nor the moment or the excitement experienced in such a situation. Perhaps you're thinking about the moment when José Mourinho threw his coat, or when he threw his medal, or when he did a lap of honour around the pitch with the UEFA Cup in his arms. I hope one day to win a cup so that I can do a lap around the pitch." The truth of the matter is that a year later Villas-Boas won the Europa League and didn't do a lap of honour around the pitch with the cup held high, as Mourinho had – perhaps simply to avoid such comparisons.

The only difference between both incidents, is that months later Mourinho's coat was auctioned on eBay for over 200,000 Euros, while Villas-Boas's blazer is probably hanging in some closet in Coimbra, perhaps waiting for that significant increase in value that Villas-Boas's work at Chelsea may bring to its current owner.

Equalling José Mourinho's place in the heart of Chelsea fans is no easy task. It was a strong, intense and emotional relationship. To such an extent that at the end of the first season even Mourinho's coat had become a cult object. The Portuguese manager wore it simply because he was cold, but the victories deified it so much that, as we have said, it could be auctioned on the Internet. All the proceeds were given to CLIC Sargent, an institution that supports children with cancer, and of which Mourinho was a patron. Chelsea were later able to recover the coat and exhibited it in the club's museum, where it remains until this very day. The mark of Mourinho runs deep, be it in terms of titles or even a simple coat. In this regard, André Villas-Boas still has a very long way to go.

Another similarity between both men is that they do not like to expose their families to media attention. At the beginning of his career, Mourinho was still being photographed in public with his family – for example, posing alongside the UEFA or Champions League Cups, or later celebrating Chelsea's first title on the turf at Stamford Bridge. But nowadays, he chooses to shelter his family more than ever from the public eye. As for André Villas-Boas, the public have never seen photographs of his family, not even in connection with his sporting victories. Consequently very few people have any idea what his wife and daughters look like. In this respect, he is even "stricter" than Mourinho.

A DIFFERENT IMPETUS

"Referees of the world will not be delighted at the prospect of another José Mourinho in their midst."

This could be read in the pages of the *Evening Standard*, in March 2005 and referred to none other than André Villas-Boas. The comment was made following the rather impetuous reaction of the then young scout, aged 27, at the end of a match between Chelsea and Barcelona during the Champions League. Chelsea had knocked out Barça at Stamford Bridge (4-2) in the thrilling match that we mentioned earlier in the book. At the end of the game André Villas-Boas had an angry confrontation with Frank Rijkaard.

Time has proven, however, that this was an isolated act. Villas-Boas rarely loses his temper. He celebrates goals exuberantly, and follows the plays intensely – but that is it. In this regard, Mourinho is much more emotional, and in some cases even provocative. There is, for example, a famous photograph of *El Especial* running on the pitch at the Nou Camp, ecstatically celebrating Inter reaching the Champions League Final after knocking out Barcelona, the title holders. Amid much jumping and laughter, he even shared the moment with the Nerazzurri fans seated in the stands. Unsurprisingly this was interpreted as an act of gratuitous provocation by many and the Catalan goalkeeper, Victor Valdés, tried to put an end to Mourinho's celebrations. It is highly improbable that André Villas-Boas will approach things in quite the same way.

Nor is it likely that he will tell his opponents' supporters to keep quiet, as Mourinho did to the Liverpool fans when he was manager at Chelsea. Nor will the Blues' new manager behave the way Mourinho did when Real Madrid visited the San Siro: he responded to the boos from the Milan fans by raising three fingers, symbolising the historic treble that he had achieved for Inter the previous season. Emílio Butragueño, Real Madrid's Director of Institutional Relations, tried to give an explanation and justification for this when he said that "Mourinho is not in football to make friends, he's in it to win".

Villas-Boas doesn't react like this. In the same way that on the pitch he is unlikely to come up with the apparently spontaneous actions that José Mourinho does on occasion. For example, in 2007, when after losing to Arsenal and waving goodbye to any chance Chelsea had of retaining the League title, Mourinho walked across the pitch to the Chelsea fans and pushed his chin up with the palm of his right hand, as if asking the supporters to leave the stadium in the same way the team would, with their heads held high. With this gesture, Mourinho was already preparing for the FA Cup Final which was to take place a fortnight later. The effectiveness of this gesture was seen when the players won the Cup and celebrated by pushing their chins up with the palm of their hand. These are the sort of reflex actions that make José Mourinho unique in his profession.

As far as many journalists are concerned both the "teacher" and the "disciple" have identical attitudes, but different characteristics. Both place a great deal of importance on press conferences, both have the gift of communicating, and both are able to convey their message effectively. Like all good "manipulators" of information, both Mourinho and Villas-Boas choose two or three ideas they want to convey – they focus on a few key phrases – and then lead the journalists towards those objectives. The headlines of the day almost always reflect the messages the two men want to emphasise.

They are prepared for every question and often have surprising answers. Nevertheless, in terms of content, one detail sets them apart: Villas-Boas is more emotional, transparent and, perhaps, genuine whilst Mourinho is colder, more calculating and more prone to staging things. And so, the Real Madrid manager is better at exploiting these meetings with journalists than Villas-Boas, using each press conference like a veritable Swiss Army knife. Not only does he use them to reprimand his players, but also to provoke his opponents' managers or to send internal messages. All based on a pre-defined script that he himself has drawn up. On this level, Villas-Boas doesn't yet possess the number of tricks displayed by José Mourinho. And he probably never will; above all because Mourinho literally believes that matches begin at the pre-match press conference and only end at the post-match press conference.

With regards to exclusive interviews, they could not be any more different. José Mourinho places no barriers on these, apart from filtering the many requests he receives. In each season, across the Portuguese and foreign media, he is likely to grant a dozen or more exclusive interviews. Villas-Boas accepted a few interviews at the beginning of his career, but he stopped doing so the minute he joined FC Porto. He only speaks in the press room, where he takes all questions, and talks for as long as necessary. On the day he was presented at Chelsea, he shocked the Portuguese journalists by refusing to speak Portuguese both during and after the press conference; something that is the exact opposite of what José Mourinho has always done. Whether in England, Italy or Spain he has always set aside five minutes to speak to the Portuguese press... in Portuguese.

And there is also the issue of the Special One versus the Group One. When André Villas-Boas was first presented to the press at Chelsea, he already knew that he would spend every day of his stay in London with the shadow of Mourinho hovering over him. He wanted to make one key difference between him and the current Real Madrid manager very clear.

When José Mourinho had been presented to the British media on his arrival at Chelsea he had said: "Please don't call me arrogant; I am a European champion and I believe I am special." And so the legend of the Special One was born.

Villas-Boas took a different approach when he set about explaining himself. "I am not the special one. Whatever the title, I'll wait for you guys to give it to me when I'm successful. I hope I am and that in the end you'll give me a good title. But this is not a one-man show." And then he explained: "This is about creating empathy, ambition and motivation in everyone. I want to group people together and be successful. Maybe I should be called "The Group One". For me, the collective is always more important than anything."

Everything that André Villas-Boas said in order to suggest that he should be seen as "the group one" could also be applied to José Mourinho. In fact, the main difference lies in the packaging, rather than in the content. In effect, Mourinho likes to be the centre of attention while Villas-Boas is more discrete in the way he does things and prefers to emphasise everyone's contribution to team victories. "In the last season, I won many things at FC Porto. This was because of the whole structure: the Board, the technical team and especially because of the players," he stated on the same occasion.

Following Porto's historic 5-0 win against Benfica at the Dragon Stadium, he had said something similar: "I must dedicate this win to my technical staff, who very often make decisions for me, since I have liberal discretion. They are decisive and essential to my work." Or, as he said after another important win against Benfica, at Luz Stadium, the one that mathematically guaranteed Porto the championship title: "These players have extraordinary talent. I want to believe I am simply a calm leader. Merit must be given to all, starting with the president, who perhaps achieved one of his most satisfying wins here. Congratulations to all, from the medical department to the scouting department, headed by Daniel Sousa, to the kit men and to everybody that works at FC Porto and at SAD (Society for Soccer Sports)."

THE SAME ROAD – DIFFERENT SHORTCUTS

The working methods of José Mourinho and André Villas-Boas are almost identical. It would be strange if they were not. They spent close on seven years together, exchanging experiences and confidences, and sharing a common plan. Nevertheless, despite the similarities in form, there are slight nuances in the content.

Villas-Boas did not attend Mourinho's training sessions on a regular basis. That was not a part of his role, and it was certainly not within the physical arena that he worked. But he did have access to the draft plans for these sessions and he helped to draw up many of them. Those who have worked with both men say that "there are obvious similarities, but Villas-Boas intervenes a lot more than Mourinho." A surprise, if we take into account that the Special One often appears to be a veritable intervention "machine".

"Villas-Boas doesn't stop drawing our attention to things, or shouting out encouragement or reprimands," says a team member who worked with both. One characteristic unites Mourinho and Villas-Boas: "Neither of them will let the assistant coach lead the training sessions: they themselves lead them, plan them and hand out the tasks," says the same source.

The Chelsea manager is meticulous in his preparation for both training sessions and matches, but not as much as the Real Madrid manager. Villas-Boas has concrete plans, but he nevertheless allows a considerable margin for imagination and improvisation. "He gives his players creative freedom." It is not by chance that he once said: "Football is chaotic and that's what makes it a special sport". Thus, there is tactical discipline, but it does not assume the letter of the law. AVB knows that a match is full of surprises. An unexpected mistake by the goalkeeper, a goal in the first minute... these are uncontrollable variables that can lay waste to any rigid tactical strategy or discipline. This is where Plan B comes in – previously discussed among the players, during training – the art of improvisation. "He wants players to carry out their roles, but he also constantly asks for creativity," which, it must be said, "only works with intelligent players. That's what happened at FC Porto."

The famous reports on the opposing teams were viewed differently – both in terms of importance and the way they were used by both managers. José Mourinho surprised his players when he arrived at FC Porto and started handing out detailed information to them about their opponents. Every player knew, exactly, the characteristics of the opponent they were to be up against. And although it was Villas-Boas who was responsible for writing up all that information, strangely enough as a manager he prefers to treat this type of data in a different way. He does not disregard it – as he confirmed upon arriving at Chelsea: "They are things that can make a difference, but whether or not they play a decisive role in the matches, nobody knows: sometimes they do, sometimes they don't"

– but he uses the information differently. Instead of focussing on the opponents' strengths, and therefore putting the players on the alert, he prefers to do this exercise the other way around: he explains to his players how their qualities can cancel out their opponents' abilities. The end result will be more or less the same, but in Villas-Boas's case there is a plus: by enumerating the qualities of his players, the manager increases their sense of pride and motivation. "The opponent is always analysed in the last talk, the technical talk, which usually takes place shortly before the match," says a player who has worked with him.

Pedrinho was one of those players. Coached by Villas-Boas at Académica, the right back draws attention to the manager's concern to include the players in the decision-making process. "He would always ask us if we were comfortable with the tactical plans used," he says. Being close to the players is a trademark of the current Chelsea manager. He himself confirmed this on the day he was presented to the club: "We are open (to the players), to their problems; and not only the problems they face on the pitch but also to the problems they face in their day-to-day life. That's the approach I want to have at this club." Orlando, also from Académica, confirms this: "He spoke to us about everything, often about things unrelated to football, and he always showed an interest in us."

This was true with Miguel Pedro, as was mentioned earlier in the book. After the death of his Pedro's twins Villas-Boas was tireless in trying to support him. This is similar to Mourinho, who also builds very close relationships with his players. It is public knowledge that after suffering serious injuries, both César Peixoto and Derlei were able to count on the manager's unconditional support – even in the operating room. Mourinho and Villas-Boas foster a certain family spirit, and consider it essential both for group unity and for ultimate success.

After a few weeks of working with André Villas-Boas, John

Terry, captain of Chelsea, confirmed some similarities between the two: "José didn't like anyone getting close to the players. We had a good relationship with him but there were days you wouldn't have gone near him. You could have a laugh and a joke with José and that could change the following day. André is very much the same now as a manager."

However, when it comes to publicly managing players' behaviour, they are completely different. Mourinho does not refrain from criticising players, sometimes very harshly, and even uses this procedure as a mechanism to balance the group. This happened, for instance, during his time at Inter Milan when he was questioned about Balotelli's behaviour: "If someone trains alongside Zanetti and Cambiasso and he doesn't learn then it must mean that he only has one neuron!" It would be unthinkable to hear this type of comment from Villas-Boas. The current Chelsea manager doesn't leave anything unsaid, but he prefers to resolve problems at "home", in discrete and private conversations.

4-3-3 – A COMMON TACTIC

Were Mourinho and Villas-Boas to still exchange views on football on a regular basis, as they did in the past, they would certainly agree on one point: the most effective tactical system is 4-3-3.

The FC Porto of 2003 – Mourinho's first – played this way. As did the FC Porto of 2011, coached by Villas-Boas. Both won the Europa League/UEFA Cup. Many specialists on the subject – including commentator Luís Freitas Lobo – say that the 2003 team was José Mourinho's best, "in terms of aesthetic seduction". The high pressure 4-3-3 became famous, with the midfield enchanted by Deco's talent.

It is worth reflecting again on some of the comments that Luís Freitas Lobo made in his foreword, exploring how Porto teams differed under the two managers. "Villas-Boas didn't have a player like Deco but he had an increased defence-attack-defence movement with Moutinho. The importance given to the defensive midfielder was similar, but Villas-Boas aimed for him to 'play more' when in possession of the ball."

A key element in José Mourinho's strategy was to have a roaming forward winger who liked to make diagonal runs. Derlei was the man Mourinho handed this task to, while Villas-Boas relied on Hulk, "different players... but they both allowed similar ways to set up a team and its attacking dynamics."

"Mourinho's full-backs defended better. Those of Villas-Boas tended to break forward more, so as to unbalance the opponent rather than to provide support."

At FC Porto, Villas-Boas didn't have a centre-back 'à la Porto' capable of exercising an authoritative voice identical to that of Jorge Costa, as Mourinho did. "André made up for that by working with two centre-backs for an increased sense of positional stability," observes Luís Freitas Lobo. At Chelsea, with the presence of John Terry, the problem of having a commanding voice at the back is not an issue.

We will never know if a second year of Villas-Boas at FC Porto would have led the manager to change to a 4-4-2 diamond shape, as Mourinho did in his second season, the one in which he won the Champions League. As Luís Freitas Lobo notes in his foreword he believed that that would have happened: "Clues in several of his games on the Porto bench indicated a wilingness, on occasion, to play with four midfielders, or more accurately, four men in midfield. And so, rather than looking to 'dominate' a game he sought (and managed) to 'control' it."

The semi-final Europa League match against Villarreal was emblematic due to the erroneous tactical interpretations of the analysts. After a passable first half, a transfigured FC Porto returned for the second half. Analysts were quick to say that Villas-

Boas had altered his tactical scheme: from 4-3-3 to 4-1-4-1, with his defence holding a high line upfield. André read the commentaries and smiled. Days later he explained to journalists that he had not made any tactical alterations. "The team played the entire game as 4-3-3," he said. The players also confirmed that their manager had only asked them to play as well as they knew how. That was the only alteration. As Freitas Lobo adds, "more than playing in different systems, what is important is to know how to change systems throughout the match".

PHILOSOPHIES

Manuel Sérgio, José Mourinho's former professor and confidante of André Villas-Boas, is in a privileged position to analyse both personalities. With a philosophical basis as his starting point, the academic recalls words written by Roger Garaudy – also a philosopher – in his book *Appel Aux Vivants*. This provides a framework for his commentary: "If competitiveness is the law in our society, why should it not be the law in my personal life?"

It is in this world, guided by frenetic competition and profit that Mourinho and Villas-Boas live. These truths are even more absolute in the footballing universe. The quality of both managers is unquestionable, but according to the professor, "they have yet to distinguish themselves by rejecting a culture that turns football into the reflection of the existing world of unlimited competition, and not the project for a more fraternal and more just world. They have yet to show that they are not objects of History, but rather builders of History itself. And therefore capable of being fraternal, even in the arena of what is ultimately a sports entertainment industry, where competition also means envy, greed and annoyance at the success of others, as well as an uncontrollable desire for power and profit."

The philosopher holds onto a hope: "José Mourinho and André Villas-Boas will teach millions of admirers, who applaud them throughout the world, that they are great coaches because they identify themselves with a new sport, in which the law of competitiveness means, in all circumstances, 'to play with' and not 'to play against'. In sport, even our opponents are friends. Just as José Mourinho and André Villas-Boas have to be."

They are both "studious men", i.e., coaches who always keep up with the latest developments. A characteristic that Manuel Sérgio considers essential: "You either learn to theorise, or you cannot be the ideal coach." Villas-Boas learnt to study with Mourinho, "but André is capable of making his own way and being a different coach," assures the philosopher. "Especially because," he argues, "it is the man you are that triumphs in the coach you can become."

And so, what really distinguishes José Mourinho from André Villas-Boas is the nature of the man.

"José Mourinho has essential leadership qualities: a great ability to read games and the wisdom to communicate so as to motivate. Whoever has these qualities in as refined a manner as José Mourinho is a brilliant coach," emphasises the former professor of the current Real Madrid manager.

Manuel Sérgio feels that André Villas-Boas was an "intelligent and diligent" assistant who now seeks to put into practice everything he learnt from the master José Mourinho. And he in no way doubts that Villas-Boas was born to be a football coach, capable of attaining the same level as Mourinho or Guardiola: "The current Chelsea manager is not yet as successful as the managers of Real Madrid and Barcelona, but he seems to be on the right path, and what is beginning to take shape is the birth of one of the greatest coaches in the history of football."

On a philosophical level, there are more points uniting Mourinho and Villas-Boas than those separating them. Manuel Sérgio knows José Mourinho well enough to recognise that he cannot abide anyone who steals his thunder. But it is also no less true that Villas-Boas should not ignore his position of former disciple or forget what he owes intellectually to his former boss.

Once they overcome these obstacles, the philosopher has no doubts: "José Mourinho and André Villas-Boas can't help but be friends... even in top competition! This is what the Portuguese people expect of them, as well as those who see sport as an instructive environment, one of unequalled virtue."

The professor concludes that the world's best coach and the young pretender to that throne "will soon meet and embrace on Mount Olympus, home of the gods. No matter how narrow-minded or dogmatic you are, you can not fail to see this."

EPILOGUE

"There is nothing more dangerous than not taking risks."

Pep Guardiola

BARÇA IN BLUE SHIRTS?

September 2007.

At last, the long-running internal feuds between manager and owner are brought to an end. Jorge Mendes – currently FIFA's best-known agent – negotiates with Roman Abramovich and José Mourinho leaves Chelsea suddenly after three victory-filled seasons. Every possible success has been achieved, some truly unique for the club – all except one that is, winning the Champions League.

Mourinho, just like Avram Grant, Luiz Felipe Scolari and Carlo Ancelotti (Guus Hiddink left for different reasons), was a victim of Abramovich's difficulty in understanding that all the money in the world cannot buy you a cup, no matter how much you want it. From September 2007 right up until the present date, it has taken the Russian magnate four years, four managers and upwards of 60 million Euros in salaries and release agreements to understand that, although he had chosen highly regarded managers, he still could not win what he most desired.

On his appointment, the English press immediately set about calling André Villas-Boas either "Mini-Mourinho" or "The Special Two". As we have seen, he arrived at Chelsea in much the same way as Mourinho did. Does his signing then mean that the Russian billionaire recognises that he made a huge mistake in dismissing his most successful coach ever, the man who today is unanimously considered the best in the world? Will André Villas-Boas be able to live up to his hefty pay cheque with wins and spectacular football performances, which is after all Abramovich's most cherished ambition?

It is a really difficult challenge, especially now. Since Mourinho left London a new coach has emerged on the scene: Pep Guardiola, who took over Barcelona in the 2008-09 season and who has taken football to new heights, setting standards of success that were truly "impossible" or unimaginable four years ago. To the point that Barcelona simply outplayed the English champions, the great Manchester United, in the 2011 Champions League Final (after already having done so in 2009) and beat José Mourinho's Real Madrid hands down in the last Spanish League.

Throughout the 2010-11 season, FC Porto were considered by many to be the European side whose football was the closest to that played by Barcelona. "FC Porto play a fast-paced and attractive football, similar in style to Barcelona," stated Gjore Jovanovski, manager of CSKA Sofia, after his team had played against the Dragons in the Europa League. Peter Pacult, manager of Rapid Vienna, who was also up against Porto in the same competition, came to a similar conclusion: "This Porto is a mini-Barcelona; they play very well and move the ball around very well..."

Many will know of the great admiration that André Villas-Boas has for Pep Guardiola, not only because of the football played by the team, but also because of the culture of the club. The current Chelsea manager has never made a secret of this. "I am an unconditional fan of Guardiola's style of play. I like it when that team wins because I feel they reflect the way all teams should play, that unattainable perfection, and I feel they are a very special team because their football is magic," he said in November 2010, when asked to comment on the duel between the two Spanish giants, before Real Madrid's visit to the Nou Camp (Barça went on to win 5-0, the heaviest defeat in José Mourinho's career).

Villas-Boas's statement could not have been more explicit. But in the press conference following Porto's victorious Europa League Final, he again paid tribute to Pep Guardiola, saying once more how much he admired Barça's style of play and almost apologising for having won that final in such an unspectacular way. "Every day, Guardiola is an inspiration to me. Fortunately, I had the opportunity to finally meet him in February. I'm inspired not only by him, but also by his philosophy, and the philosophy of Barcelona, Cruyff and

Rinus Michels. I am only sorry that I didn't win this trophy with a better performance."

Guardiola responded to this heartfelt dedication by in turn complimenting the Portuguese manager: "From now on, I will have to draw inspiration from Villas-Boas as well."

But André Villas-Boas's pedigree as a football coach suggests he will be successful wherever he may work. The great question that now remains is: whether he will be able to replicate Barcelona's style at his new club, Chelsea, and go beyond what he achieved with FC Porto, a club with fewer resources and a squad less gifted in terms of quantity and quality.

"In the next year for sure the Champions League trophy will arrive in this club. Chelsea have been in a couple of semi-finals and also one final in recent times. I don't see why we can't go on to win it." The statement came from André Villas-Boas himself and was made just a few short days after starting work at the London club. The expectations surrounding the manager, quickly spread to the players as well, as can be clearly seen in a statement made by captain John Terry in London following the pre-season Asian tour: "He's come in and, really, from day one, he's been on the ball and on the button with us all. So we're all intrigued to see what he can bring over the next few weeks and the forthcoming season."

Will André Villas-Boas finally be able to offer Roman Abramovich what he most desires, a blue-kitted Barcelona winning the Champions League? A team that puts on a show and wins titles at the same time? The future holds the key. We must await the answer.

JOSÉ MOURINHO
MADE IN PORTUGAL

the authorised biography
by Luís Lourenço

£12.99 softback, 224 pages
ISBN: 978-0-954684-33-4

With his unmistakeable self-confidence, drive and ambition, José Mourinho made an immediate impact on English football when he became manager of Chelsea in 2004. His rise from relatively humble beginnings as assistant coach to Sir Bobby Robson to most sought-after club manager in Europe, is a fascinating and revealing story.

Long-term friend, journalist Luis Lourenço tells us about the formative years of Mourinho's career. We learn of his management skills – the way he motivates players, and his football philosophy. Mourinho himself writes of his move to Roman Abramovich's Chelsea; of his 'mind games' with Sir Alex Ferguson as Manchester United are knocked out of Europe; and his fears for his and his family's safety after receiving a death threat on the eve of what should have been the biggest night of his life.

Luís Lourenço was born in Setúbal, Portugal in 1962. With a degree in Media Studies, he has been a journalist for over 20 years. He has worked for the Portuguese television channel SIC as well as for the newspapers *O Jogo* and *O Europeu*, and has been involved with the Portuguese TSF radio station from the beginning. He has known José Mourinho from an early age.